Victory

Over Death

The Gospel of Luke

Don Pruett

Publisher: Hoot Books Publishing, 851 French Moore Boulevard, Suite 136, Abingdon VA 24211.

Scripture quotations are from the King James Version (KJV) and the New King James Version (NKJV) of the Bible.

Commentaries and Bibles used for research include:

- NIV Zondervan Study Bible Commentary, copyright 2015 by Zondervan, Grand Rapids MI. Materials used are within Zondervan's limits that do not require prior written permission for usage.
- Thompson's Chain Reference Bible (KJV), third improved edition, copyright 1934 published by B. B. Kirkbride Bible

Company, Inc., Indianapolis IN. Verses quoted in this book fall within the publisher's guidelines for usage without prior consent.

- The Thompson Chain Reference Study Bible, New King James Version (NKJV), copyright 1995, publisher B. B. Kirkbride Bible Company, Inc., Indianapolis IN. The verses quoted in this book fall within the publisher's guidelines for usage without prior consent.

Some words in (*italics*) were added for clarification purposes.

ISBN: 979-8-9860608-8-0

<u>Dedication</u>

The author was blessed to be reared by Christian parents who had five children. Our parents had a strong faith and a mutual commitment to raise their children in a Christian home. We were always glad to go to church where we learned about Christ and began developing our God-given talents.

The author's siblings have always been special as we enjoyed a close bond through the years. This book is dedicated to my three sisters and brother:

Margaret Baxter (deceased), Betty Balser, Carol Beavers, and Ken Pruett

It is amazing how each sibling has always been active in church as adults. God has blessed our family in a very special way because of our common love for Christ and each other.

Introduction to Luke

Luke wrote two New Testament Books: Luke and Acts. The book of Luke reveals God's plan of salvation through His Son, Jesus Christ. God sent Jesus from heaven to earth to re-establish sinful man with a holy and righteous God. Adam's sin in the Garden of Eden drove a wedge in man's relationship with God.

God saw the need to provide a way for us to come back to Him. It is through Jesus' death, burial, resurrection, and ascension that we find an eternal hope in God. This hope of eternal life with our Savior and loved ones motivates us to keep the faith in the worst of times.

Luke was most likely a Gentile who feared God and associated with the Jews. He worshiped God in Jewish synagogues, so he had a good understanding of the Jewish culture and practices. The book of Luke was intended for both Jews and Gentiles.

Contents

Victory Over Death

Chapter One
Good News

The good news of the gospel is about the birth, death, resurrection, and ascension of our Savior Jesus Christ. It all began with the miracle of divine conception in the Virgin Mary. The prophet Isaiah foretold of the coming birth of Christ around 740 BC. It is evident God gave this prophecy to Isaiah centuries before Christ transcended from heaven to earth. Isaiah 53 explicitly details how Jesus would come to earth, and how severely He would suffer.

Isaiah said people would not be drawn to Jesus because He was handsome. He would be despised and rejected by many men, and He would be a Man of many sorrows. He would know grief as He carried our sins and sorrows on His shoulders. He would be battered, bruised, and wounded because of our sins and transgressions. It is by His stripes we are healed from a life of sin when we accept Him as our

Lord. Isaiah says we have all gone astray, so we all need a Savior to redeem us so we can be justified and make things right with God.

Isaiah said Jesus would be led like a lamb to the slaughter, but He would not try and defend Himself before angry men who would be filled with fear and jealousy. He would always be truthful before His interrogators and He would not commit violence against any person. It was God's divine plan for Jesus to be an offering for our sins. God would look at Jesus as He suffered and be satisfied that His plan was being executed through His Son. His soul would be poured out unto death, along with the criminals who would be crucified beside Jesus. In His final breaths Jesus would make intercession for those who would crucify Him. O what a loving Savior we serve!! He bore all our sins to a painful cross of death.

Overview on the Gospel According to Luke

Colossians 4:14 says Luke was a beloved medical doctor/physician. He must have been respected by many. Luke wrote the books of Luke and Acts that record the life of Christ on earth and the planting of the first New Testament churches in Asia Minor. He wrote both books to Theophilus, an unknown person to instruct him in an orderly manner the things that had been fulfilled before their eyes. Theophilus may have been a ruler as Luke refers to him as, "most excellent" in Luke 1:3.

Luke was most likely a Gentile who had close affiliations with the Jews. He was also a traveling companion with the Apostle Paul. His purpose in writing the book of Luke was to give an eye-witness account of the life of Christ. His message is evangelistic in style. Luke wanted his account to strengthen and reconfirm the faith of early Christians on the things they had already been taught. Luke wanted every reader to fully understand the impact the birth of Christ would make on every believer. The risen Savior ushered in a new era for all who would follow Him.

The book of Luke talks about:

- Fulfilling God's promises for the plan of salvation
- Christ as our Messiah, the divine Son of God
- Holy Spirit who descended from heaven to Jesus and the apostles
- Salvation for every person who will believe on Him
- Inclusion of all outcasts and Gentiles in God's plan of redemption.

There are two very significant births foretold in the first chapter of Luke: John the Baptist and Jesus.

John the Baptist (Luke 1:8-25)

Herod was the king of Judea when a priest named Zacharias served in the temple. Elizabeth was Zacharias' wife. Both Zacharias and Elizabeth were righteous before God as they faithfully kept the commandments and ordinances of the Lord. Both of them were beyond child-bearing and Elizabeth was barren.

Zacharias and Elizabeth had both wanted a son for many years.

The priests served two weeks each year on a rotating basis in the temple, and it was Zacharias' time to serve. A priest only burned incense at the daily sacrifice once in his lifetime. Zacharias had the high honor to be in the temple to burn incense while the people were outside praying. The angel Gabriel appeared to Zacharias as he burned the incense. Zacharias saw Gabriel and was troubled and feared greatly. Gabriel told Zacharias to not be afraid, for his prayer for a child had been heard. Elizabeth would bear a son and they would call him John (*the Baptist*).

John would be great in God's eyes. He would remain pure and chaste, as he would not drink wine or strong drink. As soon as he would be born, he would be filled with the Holy Spirit. Many Jews would turn from Judaism to God because of his message about the coming Messiah. John would go before Jesus to prepare the hearts of the people for His coming. He would prepare the people so they could welcome Jesus as the Messiah when He came.

Zacharias asked the angel how this could be as he and Elizabeth were so old. Gabriel told him he stood in the presence of God who sent him to deliver the message of hope for a son. Because Zacharias questioned how this could happen, the angel told him because of his disbelief, he would be unable to speak until John was born.

The crowd outside the temple wondered why Zacharias was taking so long to come out to them. He finally came out, but he could not speak. The people concluded Zacharias had seen a vision while in the temple. After his two-week tenure as a priest, Zacharias went home to be with Elizabeth. She conceived and stayed in seclusion for five months. She finally said in Luke 1:25, "Thus the Lord has dealt with me, in the days when He looked on me, to take away my reproach among people." The Lord had worked a miracle in Elizabeth who would be the mother of John the Baptist.

Jesus' Birth Foretold (Luke 1:26-37)

Six months into Elizabeth's pregnancy, the angel Gabriel was sent by God to the town of Nazareth to a young virgin named Mary. She most likely was a teenager when Gabriel came to her. Mary was pledged to be married to Joseph who was a descendant of David. The angel told Mary she was highly favored because the Lord was with her. Mary was troubled when the angel spoke and she wondered why he had come. The angel told Mary to not be afraid as she had found favor with God.

Gabriel told Mary she would conceive and bring forth a Son and would call Him Jesus. He told Mary how her Son would be great among the people. God would give Him the throne of His father David. He would have an everlasting kingdom that would never end. Mary asked the angel how this could be as she was a virgin. He told Mary in Luke 1:35, "The Holy Ghost shall come upon thee, and the power of the Highest shall overshadow thee: therefore also that holy thing which shall be born of thee shall be called the Son of God." He told Mary that with God nothing is impossible.

Mary responded to the angel by saying, "Behold the handmaid of the Lord; be it unto me according to thy word." With these words of acceptance from Mary, Gabriel left.

Mary's Visit with Elizabeth

When word got out in the small village of Nazareth that Mary, who was unmarried, was expecting a child, the tongues must have been wagging. She no doubt was ridiculed with a harsh judgment. Mary saw a need to get out of town, so she went to visit her Aunt Elizabeth. When she arrived, Elizabeth heard Mary's voice and the babe in Elizabeth's womb leaped for joy. Elizabeth was filled with the Holy Spirit and she pronounced her blessings on Mary and her baby.

Mary glorified the Lord by reciting a song called the Magnificat in Latin. She said, "My soul doth magnify the Lord, and my spirit hath rejoiced in God my Savior." Mary fully understood how God had elevated her from a peasant girl to a level where all future generations would call her blessed. She gave God the credit for doing great things through her when she recognized how holy God is. She knew God's mercy would flow to all generations through Jesus, her little baby boy. God's strength had been made evident as He lifted her from an obscure village to a place of global prominence. Jesus would fill the hungry and deal with the rich who were insensitive to the needs of others. God would bring new hope to Israel who would recall His mercy with their Father Abraham and his seed.

Mary stayed with her Aunt Elizabeth for about three months and then returned to Nazareth. Elizabeth's son John was born and all her neighbors were filled with joy because of God's mercy on her. The Jews came to circumcise John on the eighth day according to Jewish custom, and they wanted to call him Zacharias after his father, but Elizabeth told them they would call him John.

They persisted on calling the baby Zacharias, but the father wrote on a tablet saying his name would be John. At this point Zacharias could speak once again. Fear fell on all the people throughout the hill country of Judea. They wondered what kind of child John would be.

Zacharias' Song

Zacharias was filled with the Holy Ghost and prophesied saying, "Blessed be the Lord God of Israel; for he hath visited and redeemed his people, and hath raised up a horn of salvation for us in the house of his servant David." The horn of salvation would be Jesus who would save the Israelites from their enemies and cause them to remember the holy covenant God had made with His people. They wanted to serve God fearlessly and in holiness for the rest of their life. God would save them from their enemies and forgive them of their sins.

John the Baptist would be called the prophet of the Highest; for he would go before Christ to prepare his ways. John would give the people the knowledge of salvation through remission of their sins. It was through the mercy of God that God had visited them. Jesus would bring light to those in the darkness of sin as they sat in the shadow of death. He would guide their feet on a pathway of peace that comes once we have repented and come fully to Christ. John the Baptist grew up and had a strong spirit/will. He lived in the desert until God was ready for him to deliver the message of the coming Messiah to Israel.

Hope

The birth of Jesus brings hope to every person who feels a need for a Savior. You and I can play a similar role as John the Baptist as we too can tell others about a Savior who can forgive their sins and bring peace to their hurting souls. We can tell others how Jesus is coming back some day to rapture His church so we can be ushered into our heavenly home forever. People who know Christ, know hope.

- 1 Timothy 1:1- Lord Jesus Christ which is our hope.
- Titus 2:13- Looking for that blessed hope, and the glorious appearing of the great God and our Savior Jesus Christ.

- Hebrews 6:11- We desire that every one of you do show the same diligence to the full assurance of hope unto the end.
- 1 Peter 1:3- Blessed be the God and Father of our Lord Jesus Christ, which according to his abundant mercy hath begotten us again unto a lively hope by the resurrection of Jesus Christ from the dead.

These and other Scriptures are rock solid evidence that we can only find hope in Jesus Christ. He is the only source of real hope that we cannot find in the world. His hope brings new life and purpose when we may be drifting through life without a goal or destination.

Is your hope in the Lord? Come to Him to recommit your life to Him, or to find forgiveness. When we submit humbly and turn our lives over to Christ, He can accomplish great works through us. He has the power to work beyond our human limitations. You have what it takes to be a wonderful servant of God, beyond anything you can imagine.

Divine Births

Luke chapter two records the greatest birth in the history of mankind. This little baby boy grew into manhood and became our Lord and Savior, Jesus Christ. A birth brings tremendous excitement, but His birth also brought an eternal hope for every person who decides to accept Christ as the Lord of their life. Through Jesus we know what it means to be forgiven of our sins, and also have an eternal hope of living with Him some day forever and ever.

There have been many births in royal palaces throughout the centuries. These babies grow up to later inherit an earthly throne and rule their country. They are respected by the citizens for their majestic inheritance from their forefathers. They are a part of a dynasty that has existed for many years.

Jesus, our Messiah and King of kings wasn't born in a palace. He was born in a stinking stable where the animals sheltered. Rather than having a beautiful and comfortable crib, He was laid in a manger where the animals ate their feed. He did not have royal clothing or a sanitary place to come into this world as He was wrapped in swaddling birth clothes.

<u>The Birth of Christ</u> (Luke 2:1-7)

Caesar Augustus ruled the Roman Empire that included Judea in the south and Galilee in the north. Caesar ordered a census for tax purposes so every citizen in the empire was required to register in their home jurisdiction. Every person was to go to their birth city or town to register.

Joseph took Mary from Nazareth to Bethlehem to register in the census. Joseph was a descendant of David who was born in the jurisdiction of Bethlehem. This must have been a taxing trip for Mary as it was time for her baby to be born. The distance from Nazareth to Bethlehem was about ninety miles, and Mary rode on the back of a donkey.

There were no hotel or bed and breakfast rooms for them to rent when they arrived in Bethlehem. The only available space for them to spend the night was in an animal stable. Mary gave birth to

Jesus that night. She tenderly wrapped Him in swaddling clothes and laid Him in the feed trough (*manger*).

The First to Know (Luke 2:8-20)

Outside the city limits of Bethlehem, shepherds were out in the field watching over their sheep at night. The shepherd had to protect his sheep from predators and rustlers. It was possibly a cloudless night with a canopy of millions of stars in the sky. Suddenly an angel stood by the shepherds and God's glory shined all around. The shepherds were naturally frightened from this heavenly visit.

The angels instructed the shepherds to not be afraid for they had wonderful news. They told the shepherds all people would rejoice when they also heard the good news. They announced the birth of Christ the Messiah in Bethlehem who had been born that night. This good news was prophesied in Micah 5:2. The shepherds were expecting the coming of the Messiah along with all the other Jews, but little did they know He would be born in this place at this time.

The angels told the shepherds they could find baby Jesus wrapped in swaddling clothes and lying in a manger. This would be their proof they had found the Messiah. This fulfilled the Old Testament Scriptures found in I Samuel 2:34, II Kings 19:29, and Isaiah 7:14: Then a large angelic choir from heaven joined the angels praising God and bringing glory to God in the highest heaven and tidings of peace to all men on earth.

The angels departed and went back into heaven. The shepherds decided to go to Bethlehem immediately to find this baby the angels had revealed to them. They knew the angels and the choir were from heaven, and their message was from God. The shepherds lost no time in going to find the baby lying in a manger near to Mary and Joseph. When they saw the baby, they could not contain themselves. They told about the message the angels gave them and about the fact they had seen the promised Messiah. They gave glory to God for all they had seen and heard. But Mary kept all these things to herself as she thought about all that had happened. She must have been elated and felt so blessed that she could give birth to the Son of God.

The baby was circumcised eight days after He was born according to Jewish custom and they called Him Jesus just as the angel Gabriel instructed her before she conceived.

Jesus' Dedication (Luke 22-35)

Jewish law said the mother of a newborn male baby had to go through a period of forty days of purification after the birth (Leviticus 12:1-4). Jewish male babies were required to be consecrated (*dedicated*) to the Lord. They were to sacrifice two doves or two pigeons to the Lord during the dedication service. The consecration of baby boys was in remembrance of God's sparing the lives of the first-born males in Jewish families on Passover night when they were ready to be freed from Egyptian slavery many years ago. This plague of death on Egypt was God's punishment for Pharaoh's refusal to release the Israelites from slavery. God spared the Jewish males because the parents applied the blood of a lamb on the door posts and lentils. The death angel passed over these houses where the blood of the lamb was applied. The practice of purification for the mother and consecration of the male babies re-focused their attention on God's mercy and deliverance. God had kept His promise to send a Messiah and a Savior.

There was a very devout and righteous elderly man in Jerusalem by the name of Simeon. The Israelites were awaiting God's deliverance as prophesied in the Old Testament book of Isaiah (Isaiah 40:1 and 51:3). They expected God to deliver them from spiritual, political, and emotional oppression.

The presence of the Holy Spirit in Luke 2:25 shows God's presence was upon Simeon and that God had provided His final act of salvation. The Holy Spirit had spoken to Simeon previously and promised he would not die before seeing the Messiah. Simeon was moved by the Spirit to go to the temple courts. Mary and Joseph brought Baby Jesus to Simeon for the consecration. Simeon took the baby in his arms and praised God, for he now held the Savior of the world in his hands.

Simeon told God He had kept His promise as he had now seen the Messiah. He had witnessed God's salvation in the baby he held. Jesus would be a blessing for all people of all nations and a light to the Gentiles who were considered as heathen by the Jews. The people of Israel had received a special blessing from God when Jesus was born in Bethlehem. Simeon told God He could now let him go in peace. He could die peacefully knowing he had come in direct contact with the Messiah. God had kept His promise to Simeon.

Mary and Joseph were amazed at the words Simeon spoke about Jesus. Simeon then pronounced God's blessings on Mary and Joseph. Some Jews would rise to accept Jesus while others would fall away after seeing and hearing him. People are still either drawn to or repelled by Jesus' message of forgiveness today. It is up to each individual on how to respond to the message of Christ.

Anna was an elderly prophetess in the temple.

She was married for seven years when her husband died. Anna remained a widow until she was eighty-four years old. She never left the temple, but worshiped, fasted, and prayed day and night. She came to Mary and Joseph and thanked God and told them how many had looked forward to the coming of the Messiah. She had seen how Simeon had dedicated Baby Jesus to God. He would become a special blessing to many people.

Mary and Joseph had now met the requirements of the Old Testament Law by observing the rites of purification and dedication. They returned as a family to their home in Nazareth. Jesus grew and became strong; he was filled with wisdom and the grace of God was upon him.

Jesus in the Temple (Luke 2:41-52)

Mary and Joseph traveled to Jerusalem annually to celebrate the Feast of the Passover. They took Jesus, their twelve-year-old boy with them. The celebration was over and the hordes of people headed home. Mary and Joseph did not realize Jesus had stayed in Jerusalem. After traveling all day, they started trying to find Jesus, but he was not in their traveling party. They checked with all their relatives and friends but he wasn't with them.

They went back to the city and looked for Jesus for three days. They finally found him sitting in the temple courts, listening to the teachers and asking questions. The teachers were amazed at Jesus' brilliance and knowledge. Jesus' parents asked Him why he stayed behind because they were so concerned about his safety. Jesus asked them why they had been searching for him as he had to be in His Father's house and occupied with His Father's business.

They took Jesus home with them, but they did not fully understand what He told them. Jesus obeyed what His parents told him. Mary was a deep-thinker and kept Jesus' sayings in her heart as she pondered just how special He was. Jesus continued to get taller and wiser as He found favor with both God and man.

God sent His Son from heaven to earth for one single reason: to seek and to save the lost. He came to rescue us from the slavery of sin and give us salvation.

John the Baptist's Message (Luke 3:2-20)

John the Baptist was living in the desert when God spoke to him with instructions for his ministry and the message he was to preach to the people. He preached baptism of repentance for the remission of sins. The people's remorse for their sins caused some to repent and be baptized for the remission (*cancellation of a sin debt*). The prophet foretold in Isaiah 40:3-5 about how there would be one who would tell the people to prepare the way of the Lord and make His paths straight. All flesh would see God's salvation when Jesus started His ministry.

John the Baptist did not mince words or sugar-coat sin. He called the crowd that came to be baptized a brood of vipers. He plainly told them they needed to repent of their sins. They could not take comfort in being one of Abraham's descendants as they each needed to deal with the sin in their life. He referred to the people as trees when he told them all unfruitful trees would be cut down and cast into the fire. John's message resonated with them and they asked him what they should do. He told them to share what they had with the needy. John told the tax collectors who came to be baptized to not collect more taxes from the people than the designated amount due. John told the soldiers to not intimidate anyone or make false charges.

They began to question in their minds if John the Baptist was actually Christ. John quickly told them he came to baptize with water, but One mightier was coming. John told them he was not even worthy to unfasten the straps on Jesus' sandals. He told them the One who would come shortly would baptize with the Spirit and fire. We receive the gift of the Holy Spirit at baptism (*Acts 2:38*). At the Last Day, Jesus will separate the good people (*the saved*) from the bad (*unsaved*). The saved will be ushered in to eternal life, and the unsaved will be cast into an eternal fire. Herod had John locked up in prison because of his brutally honest message.

Oh, what a Savior!

Chapter Two
Baptism and Temptation

<u>Jesus' Baptism</u> (Luke 3.21-22)

All four Gospel writers recorded the event of Jesus' baptism by John the Baptist. He was baptizing several people in the Jordan River when Jesus appeared. In John 1:29, John saw Jesus coming and said, "Behold, the Lamb of God who takes away the sins of the world!" He recognized Jesus as God's Son and His power to forgive all men of all sin if we come to Him in repentance.

When He was baptized, Jesus prayed and the heavens opened. The Holy Spirit came down from heaven in bodily form like a dove and lit on Jesus. A voice came from heaven and said, "You are My beloved Son; in You I am well pleased" (Luke 3:22). The prophet said in Isaiah 11:1-2 that a rod would come out of the stem of Jesse and a Branch (*Christ*) would grow out of his roots. The Spirit would rest upon Him (*Christ*). The Spirit would bring wisdom, understanding, counsel, might, knowledge, and the fear of the LORD. The Holy Spirit still imparts these things to every baptized believer.

Baptism was obviously very important to Jesus. The subject should not be debated among men since the Bible clearly teaches us the importance of being baptized. Several verses confirm the fact that baptism is a requirement and not an option:

- Matthew 28:19– Jesus told His apostles to go make disciples in all the nations, baptizing them in the name of the Father, the Son, and the Holy Spirit.
- Mark 16:16– He who believes and is baptized will be saved; but he who does not believe will be condemned.
- John 3:5– Jesus said unless one is born of water and the Spirit, he cannot enter the kingdom of God.
- Galatians 3:27– We put on Christ when we are baptized.

Luke then gives a thorough genealogy of Jesus Christ. He most likely drew on the information contained in the Old Testament books of Genesis

5:1-32, Genesis 11:10-26, Ruth 4:18-22, and 1 Chronicles 1:1-4. Luke traces Jesus' ancestors and their blood lines through famous men. Some of Jesus' earthly ancestors included Joseph, Levi, Amos, Nathan, David, Jesse, Jacob, Isaac, Abraham, Noah, and Adam. Jesus inherited this Jewish legacy when He came from heaven to earth.

Jesus' Temptations (Luke 4:1-11)

Matthew, Mark and Luke all wrote about how severely Jesus was tempted after His baptism. He was led by the Holy Spirit into the wilderness to be tempted for forty days by the devil. Jesus fasted without food and prayed while in the wilderness. He often went to be alone with the Father to gain heavenly strength and to be certain He was doing God's will every day; consequently, He lived a sinless life on earth. But this did not mean Satan would not tempt Christ. Every Christian is Satan's target as it is his intent to draw us away from Christ.

Satan tried to lie and deceive Christ by tempting him with the lust of the flesh, the lust of the eyes, and the pride of life. Satan still uses these three major types of temptation on us today.

- Lust of the flesh– He tempted Jesus to turn the stones into bread (Luke 4:3).
- Lust of the eyes– Satan took Jesus on a high mountain and showed Him all the visible kingdoms. He lied and told Christ he had been given authority over the kingdoms, and he would give them to Christ if He would worship him (Luke 4:5 – 8).
- Pride of Life– He took Jesus to the temple in Jerusalem and sat Him on the high gable. He told Jesus if He was the Son of God to cast Himself down and the angels would guard over Him, bear Him up, and keep Him from being dashed on the stones (Luke 4:9-11).

Jesus resisted Satan on each temptation by quoting from the book of Deuteronomy.

- When He was tempted to turn the stones to bread, Jesus told Satan that man shall not live by bread alone, but by every word that comes from the mouth of God (Deuteronomy 8:3).

- When Satan offered all the visible kingdoms to Christ, He told Satan to get behind Him because he should worship the LORD God, and Him only (Deuteronomy 6:13).
- Jesus' response to Satan when He sat on the temple gable was, "You shall not tempt the LORD your God." (Deuteronomy 6:16)

It is important to note that Satan, a fallen angel whom God expelled from heaven had no authority over Jesus the Son of God. Christ was given power over heaven and earth by God and Satan was trying to get Christ to believe he had more authority. He used deceit and lies on Christ, but Jesus resisted Satan each time. Christ has given us the example we too can follow to resist Satan by quoting these same scriptures He used. At this point Satan left Jesus alone as he saw Christ would not fall for his evil scheme.

<u>Jesus Launches His Ministry</u> (Luke 4:14 – 30)

The Holy Spirit descended on Jesus when He was baptized. He went back to Galilee filled with the power of the Holy Spirit. His fame spread quickly throughout the entire region. There had never been a person in their midst like Jesus. He began teaching in the Jewish synagogues, and many were pleased to be in Jesus' presence.

Jesus returned to His hometown in Nazareth on the Sabbath, and He stood to read the prophecy in the scroll about Himself from Isaiah 61:1-2. This prophecy was written several hundred years before the birth of Christ. Isaiah wrote about the coming Messiah, "The Spirit of the Lord God is upon me; because the LORD hath anointed me to preach good tidings unto the meek; he hath sent me to bind up the brokenhearted, to proclaim liberty to the captives, and to open the prison to them that are bound; to proclaim the acceptable year of the LORD, and the day of vengeance of our God; to comfort all that mourn."

Jesus was anointed and appointed by God to come from heaven to earth to do all these things for the poor, the sick, the bereaved, and the incarcerated. We may be bruised and battered from life's trials and afflictions, but Jesus came to bring comfort and hope regardless of our circumstances. Every person has access to what Christ has to offer, no matter what hand we have been dealt.

Jesus rolled up the scroll of Isaiah and sat down. Everyone in the synagogue was looking at Him. They knew He was a very special person. Jesus told them the Scripture (*from Isaiah*) had been fulfilled in their presence that day. The people were amazed at the words He spoke and questioned each other if He was Joseph's Son.

Jesus told them no prophet is acceptable and welcome in his own town. He told them about the many widows in Israel during the days of Elijah when a famine came. The famine lasted three and one-half years in all the land. Elijah was sent to a widow in Sidon. When Elijah first met the widow, she was picking up sticks to build a fire so she could bake bread for her and her son. Her barrel of meal and cruse of oil had run out and she only had enough left so the two of them could eat their final meager meal and then die from starvation.

Elijah told the woman to give him some bread and it was then that she announced her predicament. Elijah insisted she bake the bread for him first and then make bread for her and her son. She obeyed Elijah and because of her deep faith in what he had told her, the supply of meal and oil was replenished constantly until the famine ended.

There were many lepers in Israel, and none of them except Naaman was healed by Jesus. The people were enraged and drove Him out of town; they were ready to throw Jesus over a nearby high cliff, but He passed through the crowd and left town.

Jesus' Power Over Evil Spirits (Luke 4:31-37)

Jesus came down to the town of Capernaum in Galilee where he taught the people on the

Sabbath days. They too were amazed at His teaching; for He spoke with authority and power. The Holy Spirit was already at work in Jesus' young ministry.

There was a man in the synagogue who was possessed with a demonic spirit. He cried out with a loud voice and Jesus heard him. The evil spirits in the man asked Jesus to leave them alone. They knew how powerful Jesus was and they wanted to know if He had come to destroy them. They acknowledged He was holy and was from God. Jesus commanded the evil spirit to come out of the man. The spirit threw the man on the floor and came out of him. The witnesses were astonished at what Jesus had done. They recognized his power and authority over the evil spirits. Jesus still has power over Satan and all his evil angels that roam the earth seeking whom they may devour.

<u>Healing Power</u> (Luke 4:38-41)

Jesus then went to Simon Peter's house where Peter's mother-in-law was burning up with a high fever. The family pleaded with Jesus to do something to break the fever. Jesus rebuked the fever, and it left her. She immediately got up and started waiting on her family. Jesus' power over every situation in life is to never be ignored or minimized. He is all-powerful over every problem that can befall us. We must come in repentance for our sins and seek His will in our bad situation. When we pray for His will to be done, things can change quickly. When our hearts are right with God, we are then prepared to accept His will.

That evening when the sun set on the Sabbath Day, all who had friends or family who were sick brought them to Jesus for healing. He laid His hands on each of them and cured every disease. Some were demon-possessed, and they too came out screaming about Jesus being the Son of God. Jesus rebuked and silenced the evil spirits because the spirits knew He was the divine Son of God. Jesus gives us the power through the Holy Spirit to also rebuke and resist the devil, but we must be pro-active to be successful.

On Sunday morning, Jesus left Peter's house and went into isolation in the desert. The people found Jesus and tried to keep Him from leaving, but Jesus had work to do. He told them He had to preach the good news of the Gospel. He told them this was His purpose in coming to earth so He could spread the good news. He continued preaching and teaching in the synagogues in Galilee.

Jesus still has the power to help us deal with the problems of life. He has the power over all problems including sadness, finances, dysfunctional families, illness, stress, and incarceration. Jesus may not remove the problem, but He can empower us to endure the problem. We depend on Him to minister to us through the power He gives to the Holy Spirit.

<u>Chapter Three</u>
The Call of Jesus

<u>Calling Disciples </u>(Luke 5:1-11)

The task facing Jesus to spread the Gospel to as many people in a short period of time required some co-workers. Jesus only had three short years to complete His ministry on earth, and He knew He could reach people more quickly if He had dedicated disciples working by His side. The men Jesus selected were not qualified for ministry based on human terms; they had never gone to seminary or prepared a sermon.

These were ordinary men who were commercial fishermen, tax collectors, etc. but Jesus taught them with on-the-job training as they worked side-by-side with Him. Eleven of the twelve men were totally dedicated to Christ. Unfortunately, Judas Iscariot was a traitor who later led the soldiers at night to Christ so they could arrest Him. Jesus used Judas to fulfill the scripture that prophesied His betrayal.

Jesus was standing by the Lake of Gennesaret (*Sea of Galilee*) with a crowd pressing in on Him. Jesus saw two boats on the shore, but the fishermen were not on the boats as they were washing their nets in the edge of the water. Jesus got into Simon Peter's boat, and He asked Peter to pull the boat a short distance from the shore where He sat in the boat and taught the people.

Then Jesus told Peter to put the boat in deeper water and lower his nets for a haul. Peter told Jesus they had worked hard all night and had not caught any fish. They were no doubt tired as they had toiled all night only to pull in empty nets. Peter said they would lower their nets simply because that is what Jesus told them to do. They caught so many fish the nets were about to break. They filled both boats until they were about to sink because they followed Jesus' simple instructions. Sometimes we rationalize that we have done all we know to do to win others to Christ on our own. We need to turn those who have refused our message over to the Lord and ask Him to intervene.

Peter asked Jesus to depart from him for he was a sinful man. The men were amazed they had caught so many fish after catching nothing all night. Jesus told Peter, James, and John to not be afraid for He would make them fishers of men (Luke 5:9-11). These three men soon became Jesus' inner-circle among the twelve disciples. The men rowed the two boats ashore and left everything they had accumulated in their fishing business so they could join forces with Jesus in His full-time ministry.

Jesus' Power to Heal (Luke 5:12-26)

Leprosy was a highly contagious, infectious disease caused by a bacterium. It affected the body tissues including the skin, nerves, and mucous membranes. Lepers were considered as outcasts as they could no longer go to work or live with their families. They had to live in leper's colonies with others who suffered the same disease. Leprosy is transferred among humans through droplets from the nose and mouth, much like COVID and other infectious diseases. There was no known cure for leprosy in Jesus' day. These victims lived without hope or purpose since leprosy had delivered a death sentence.

One day Jesus met a man whose skin was covered with leprosy. He fell on his face before Jesus and begged him to cure him and make him clean if the Lord was willing. Jesus touched the man and told him He was willing, and to be cleansed. Jesus told him to tell no one until he showed himself to the priest. He was to give an offering as proof and evidence of his healing. This command was first made in Leviticus 13:49.

Good news spreads quickly and large crowds came to Jesus to hear Him and to be healed. Jesus withdrew to the desert and prayed. This could have been a prayer of thanksgiving to God for giving Him healing power; or it could have been a prayer asking God to restore His strength.

On another occasion, Jesus taught the Pharisees and teachers of the Law who had come from all over the kingdom to Jerusalem. They wanted to be with Jesus and be healed. The power of God was upon Jesus who could bring healing in humanly impossible situations. Jesus was teaching a standing-room-only crowd.

Some men brought a paralyzed man to Jesus for healing, but they could not get through the crowd. They took the man up on the roof, removed some of the roof tiles, and lowered his stretcher down to Jesus. He saw their faith and confidence that caused them to think and act outside the box. Because of their faith and determination, He forgave the man his sins. The scribes and Pharisees began arguing and asking each other who this man was who spoke blasphemies against God. How dare anyone to forgive sins like He was God!

Jesus could read their thoughts and minds and He asked them why they questioned what He did. Then Jesus asked them if it was easier to forgive sins or to heal the paralytic man. He told them He had the power and authority to forgive sins. He told the paralyzed man to pick up his stretcher and go home. The man obeyed Christ and picked up his stretcher and went home as

Jesus commanded. He praised and thanked God for healing.

Some in the crowd were amazed at what Jesus did to forgive the man's sins and heal him. They thanked God and praised Him with a reverential fear. They had seen wonderful, strange, and unthinkable things that day.

Calling Matthew (Luke 5:27-32)

Jesus then went out and saw Matthew (*Levi*), a tax collector sitting in his office. Jesus told Matthew to come and be His disciple. Matthew had an important job and he could have told Jesus he could not give up his lucrative position with the Roman government to follow Him. He made a nice living collecting taxes on a commission basis for Rome. Jesus was asking a lot of Matthew to give up his nice job and good income.

But Matthew was drawn to Jesus. He willingly gave up his career so he could work with Christ. Matthew threw a celebration party at his house for his friends and other tax collectors. They had a nice meal together with Christ that day. The Pharisees and scribes grumbled and complained that Jesus and His disciples were eating with tax collectors and sinners. Jesus told them those who are healthy don't need a physician, but those who are sick. Jesus made it clear He did not come to invite righteous people but sinners who needed to repent of their sins. Jesus wanted the sinners to change their hearts and minds as they recognized sin and its consequences. He wanted them to hate their sins and love Him.

The grumblers and complainers told Jesus that John's disciples fasted and prayed often while His disciples ate and drank with sinners. This was an opportunity for Jesus to teach them a parable.

Jesus told them wedding guests would not fast as long as the bridegroom was with them, but one day the bridegroom would leave and then they could fast and pray. Jesus, our Bridegroom, was with them a short while before He returned to His Father in heaven. He told them further that no one puts a new patch on an old garment because it would tear the garment. The new patch would not match the old, faded garment. Then Jesus told them that no one pours new wine into an old wineskin because the wine would burst the skin. New wine must be placed into fresh pliable skins. Likewise, no one wants to drink new wine after drinking aged and mature wine.

The meaning behind this parable was to open the eyes of the scribes and Pharisees that a transition was taking place between the period of the Old Testament Law and the New Testament era of God's grace and mercy. Jesus is the central figure as He came from heaven to fulfil the old Law and usher in grace and mercy. The Ten Commandments were written on tablets of stone, but in the new era Jesus' commands are written on our hearts. Jesus was telling them to not try to mix the old with the new.

Jesus is Lord (Luke 6:1-5)

Jesus and His disciples walked through a field of standing grain on the Sabbath (*Saturday*). The disciples picked some of the grain heads and rubbed the chaff away so they could eat the grain. The Law said it was legal to pick the grain heads without an instrument, but when they rubbed the grain they were breaking the Law because this constituted work that was forbidden under their Sabbath Law.

The Pharisees watched every move Jesus made. They saw what the disciples did and told Jesus that it was unlawful for them to do this on the Sabbath (Exodus 20:10). Jesus asked the Pharisees if they had read how David went into the house of God and ate the sacred loaves of shewbread (1 Samuel 21:1-6, Leviticus 24:9). Only the priests were permitted to eat the shewbread, but David and his companions all ate the forbidden shewbread. Jesus told the Pharisees He is the Lord even of the Sabbath. Jesus did not come to break but to fulfill the Old Testament Law. He let them know it was proper for the disciples to fill their hunger on the Sabbath.

The Sabbath Law (Luke 6:6-11)

Jesus never backed down in spite of accusations from the Pharisees. He was in the synagogue on the Sabbath as the Pharisees and scribes watched His every move. A man whose right hand was withered was in the synagogue. The Pharisees watched closely to see if Jesus would heal on the Sabbath. They wanted to catch Him healing on the Sabbath so they could accuse Him of breaking the Old Testament Law. It had not sunk in that Jesus came to fulfil the Law, not break it or do away with it.

Jesus knew very well the intentions of the Pharisees. He told the man with the withered hand to come forward, so he came and stood before Him. Jesus looked the Pharisees in the eye and asked them if it was lawful and right to do good or evil and to save a life or destroy it. The Pharisees did not respond. He told the man to hold out his hand, and when he did, his hand was fully restored. The Pharisees were filled with lack of understanding and were indignant toward Jesus. They discussed what they could do to Him. The Pharisees were more concerned about the legal aspects of the Law than the man whose hand had been healed.

The fact that Jesus performed a miracle in their presence meant nothing; for He had broken the Law of the Sabbath in their opinion. God gave Jesus the power to heal. He placed His stamp of approval by allowing Jesus to have the power to heal every day including the Sabbath. Jesus never claimed healing power as every miracle He performed was done through the power of God (John 14:10).

<u>Jesus Chooses Twelve Disciples</u> (Read Luke 6:12-16)

Jesus needed co-workers to help Him in His earthly ministry. There is power when people join hands to work together in a common cause, and this was no different in Jesus' ministry. Jesus went into a mountain where he prayed to God all night. He was seeking God's guidance before selecting His twelve disciples. The next morning he called all His disciples and from the large group, He selected the twelve who would labor alongside Him. Most of these men were very ordinary men who had no formal education in ministry. Jesus would teach them each day as He confronted different people and situations. One of the twelve Jesus selected was Judas Iscariot who would later betray Him before His arrest and crucifixion. The betrayal was to fulfill Old Testament prophecy (Psalm 41:9).

These disciples learned from Jesus with on-the-job training. These men, plus Paul, would later be elevated from disciples (*learners*) to apostles (*the sent*). They would go out to evangelize the known world teaching repentance, confession, and baptism. The apostles planted New Testament churches in many cities where they preached.

Jesus and His disciples came down from the mountain to a level field where many disciples had gathered to hear Him teach. They had come from all over Judea, Jerusalem, Tyre, and Sidon. Many in the crowd had various diseases and ailments; there were even some who were possessed with unclean spirits. Jesus healed them all and drove out the evil spirits. He showed His power over disease and Satan's evil work by taking control of people. They all wanted to touch Jesus since healing power was flowing in a mighty way.

The summary for this chapter is:

- Jesus uses ordinary people who are untrained and unprepared to do His kingdom work today.
- Jesus still has healing power if it is His will.
- He called twelve disciples then, just as He calls us into service today.

What is Jesus calling us to do? Do we love Him with all our soul, heart, and being? Are we showing love to our neighbor as He commanded? There is something He is calling every one of us to do. What is He calling you to do? Are you ready to take that step of faith?

Chapter Four
Jesus' Teaching and Warning

<u>The Beatitudes</u> (Matthew 5:1-12, Luke 6:20-26)

Jesus went up on a mountain and sat down. His disciples and a large crowd of followers came up to hear Him teach. He pronounced His blessings on people with different virtues or qualities. The traits Jesus taught rarely brought acclaim or fame but were for the faithful and true. This lesson focuses on those who already believe in Christ as the Son of God. We find blessings or happiness by using our good qualities for Jesus. When we are happy in Jesus we are content and spiritually prosperous. We know joy and satisfaction because of God's favor and salvation.

In Matthew 5:3-11, Jesus taught the Beatitudes to His disciples (*learners*). We can interpret the word "blessed" with the word "happy." These blessings from Christ are His recipe for happiness in this world:

- Blessed/happy are the poor in spirit for theirs is the kingdom of heaven! These are the humble who feel insignificant as servants of God.
- Blessed/happy are those who mourn for they shall be comforted! We mourn over losses and past sins. We can find happiness and peace even when we mourn for our trust is in the Lord to comfort and forgive. We rest in His matchless grace in our worst moments. One day our weeping will be turned into joy.
- Blessed/happy are the meek, for they shall inherit the earth! The meek are the patient, mild, and long-suffering who are content with what they have.
- Blessed/happy are those who hunger and thirst after righteousness, for they shall be filled! Every believer should have a hunger and thirst to be as righteous as we can be before the God who created us. When we are spiritually hungry or thirsty, we turn to God's Word to learn more about Him so our spiritual hunger can be satisfied.

- Blessed/happy are the merciful, for they shall obtain mercy! When we extend mercy to others, we show our compassion for their plight.
- Blessed/happy are the pure in heart, for they shall see God! He expects us to live pure and righteous lives as we reflect God's love to others. There is no hint of hypocrisy when our hearts are pure.
- Blessed/happy are the peacemakers, for they shall be called the sons of God! The world needs more peacemakers and fewer troublemakers. Peacemakers are called sons of God.
- Blessed/happy are those who are persecuted for righteousness' sake, for theirs is the kingdom of heaven! Many are persecuted because of their faith in God, but they are promised permanent residence in heaven. Then we will never fear persecution because of our faith.
- Blessed/happy when they revile and persecute you and say all kinds of evil against you falsely for My sake. Rejoice and

be exceedingly glad, for great is your reward in heaven, for so they persecuted the prophets who were before you! We take the high road when criticized, and this is a testimony of our commitment to Christ. The reward for suffering for Christ's sake awaits us in heaven.

These nine blessings come directly from the mouth of Christ to each believer. Every person most likely possesses one or more of the traits mentioned by Jesus in the Beatitudes. His blessings are available in this life and the life to come. Our earthly happiness is dependent on Christ.

Men look for blessings and happiness often in the wrong places. We can pursue travel, entertainment, friendships, relationships and even work, without making Christ a part of our plan. We focus on the earthly instead of the heavenly. True and lasting happiness can only come by knowing Jesus as the Lord of our life.

A Warning (Luke 6:24-26)

Jesus knew how to talk to people in very simple and understandable terms. He didn't try to impress his listeners with confusing words. He now turns His hearer's attention from pronounced blessings of happiness to a warning.

Jesus warned the rich they were already receiving the comfort of their riches and prosperity (*achievement*). It is easy to want things that are very desirable and enjoyable. There certainly is nothing wrong with owning these things that bring temporary happiness if they do not rule our lives. However, sometimes our toys can rob us of our relationship with God if they become an idol. Anything that draws us away from the Lord is of the devil and should be avoided. Jesus warned the rich there is no heavenly reward left when we place a higher priority on our earthly stuff. Prosperity is great if it does not interfere in our relationship with God. Jesus said our earthly happiness can be turned into weeping. We cannot afford to count on earthly things to bring lasting joy and happiness.

Jesus also warns us to be aware when someone flatters us with complimentary words (*applause*). He knew flattery can feed our ego which results in pride. This is one of Satan's tools he uses to distract us in our walk of faith. We are to love those who do good, and we respect our enemies and those who hate us for our Christian walk. Jesus tells us to pray for the happiness of those who curse or abuse us. It takes a strong Christian to pray for someone who disparages and belittles our faith. By taking the high road in the face of criticism, we sow seeds of kindness that may make a difference in someone's life. We carry the banner of Christ by being more like Him, and this can cause someone to see the error of their ways.

Jesus then gives us instructions on how a Christian should behave. Some of these things may seem radical, but it is what Christ demands. He tells us if someone strikes us on the cheek to turn the other cheek. If someone steals our coat, we should also give them our shirt. We are to take care of beggars who have need for necessities. We are not to demand a return if someone steals what we have. Jesus tells us to treat others as we want to be treated. We are to love everyone, not just those who love us; this includes saints and sinners. We are to overcome other's evil deeds with kindness and respect.

We are to be helpful to all men; for if we are only kind to those who show kindness to us, this is insufficient. We are not to lend money to gain interest, for this is what sinners do. Jesus instructs us to love our enemies and those who would take advantage of us if we want a rich reward as His child. We are to show mercy and be sympathetic just like God. These are hard lessons but this sums up what a Christian should be.

Judging (Luke 6:37-42)

God has relieved us of the responsibility of judging others. If we were to judge someone, it would be based on man's standards and not God's. We are messing with a person's life when we judge them. Jesus speaks clearly when He instructs us to not judge others, lest they judge us in the same manner. We are not to condemn or pronounce guilt on anyone, but we are to acquit them of all guilt.

We are to give good gifts just as we have bountifully received them. Jesus likened our gifts to grain that has been pressed down, shaken together, and running over. The same measure we use to deal out to others will be measured back to us when we receive gifts.

Jesus used a parable when He asked them if the blind can lead the blind. If this happens, both will fall in the ditch together. A pupil is not greater than his teacher, but we learn so we can be more like our teacher. We cannot remove the speck that is our neighbor's eye before removing the beam from our own eye. If we can't see the timber in our eye, it is impossible to remove the speck of sin from our neighbor's eye. We must first deal with our sin problem before trying to help our neighbor find forgiveness for his.

A healthy tree does not bear defective or faulty fruit; likewise, an unhealthy tree cannot bear healthy fruit. Every tree is known by the kind of fruit it bears. A fig does not grow on an apple tree, nor do grapes grow on a bramble bush. An upright person produces honorable works while an evil man bears bad works. Out of the abundance of our hearts our mouth speaks.

Our Response to Jesus (Luke 6:46-49)

Jesus requires a response from every person to His offer of forgiveness and eternal life. When God created Adam, He gave man the right to choose or to reject Him— to obey or disobey. We saw how many accepted Christ while others rejected Him during His earthly ministry. They listened to Jesus teach and they watched Him perform miracles, but many still rejected Him. They were in the presence of the Son of God but elected to walk with Him no more.

Jesus asked why they called Him Lord but failed to do what He said. A person who comes to Christ and hears His words is like a builder who digs deep and lays a foundation for a house on a rock.

When the storms of life come, a spiritual house will stand because it is built on the solid rock of God's truth. In times of extreme loss, broken relationships, financial problems, family dysfunction, abuse, or neglect our spiritual house can stand because we have Christ in our life.

On the other hand, a person who hears but does not practice doing Christ's word is like a man who built a house without a proper foundation. When the storms of life blow, this man cannot survive the storm because he lacks a strong spiritual foundation. Jesus is our Rock and we can depend on Him to be by our side regardless of our circumstances.

Each of us should be able to give Jesus a quick and dedicated response to serve Him regardless of the circumstances we face. It is only in Christ that we have the assurance of victory over present day losses and set-backs. The Scriptures encourage us to hold on and persevere to the end.

Chapter Five
The Miracle Man

Jesus continued performing miracles in Luke 7. He demonstrated His God-given power over disease, death, and sin. Jesus is just as powerful today, although He does not reside bodily on earth. After He was crucified, He ascended back to God His Father in Heaven. He sits by God's throne today making intercession as our Mediator. Jesus sent the Holy Spirit to dwell in our hearts and give us daily guidance in our walk with Christ.

Jesus left the mountain in Luke 7:1-10 and went to Capernaum near the Sea of Galilee. A centurion who was a commander in the Roman army lived in Capernaum. A centurion was over 60-80 soldiers normally in a Roman legion. He could give his soldiers and servants work orders and they would carry out his wishes. The centurion's servant, who was of great value, was sick to the point of death. The centurion was a good man as he had built the local synagogue at his own expense.

The commander sent word for Jesus to come so He could heal his servant. Jesus started toward the man's house, but the centurion changed his mind and sent word that He should not come because he felt insufficient to have the Lord in his house. He asked Jesus to just speak a word of healing for the servant from where he was.

Jesus did not take offense at being un-invited to come to the centurion's house; instead, He marveled at the man's strong faith. He told the people who followed Him that He had not witnessed such strong faith in all Israel. The Jewish elders delivered their message to Christ and then returned home. When they arrived, the servant had been healed.

Sometimes Christians may feel insufficient or unworthy to even be called a child of God. We must remember a very small amount of faith can be used by God to produce a bountiful harvest. Matthew 13:31-32 says the kingdom of heaven is like a grain of mustard seed that a man sowed in his field. This smallest of seeds grew into a tree so the birds could find shelter in its branches. God can take our small and weak faith and enrich it so we can be productive instruments in His hands.

Jesus' Power Over Death (Luke 7:11-17)

Shortly after healing the servant, Jesus and a large number of disciples went to the town of Nain. Everywhere Jesus went, He found opportunities to minister to people, and Nain was no exception. As Jesus neared the gates to the town, He met a funeral procession. A widow was grieving the loss of her only son who was being carried to his burial place. Many people were in the procession and they mourned for the widow. Jesus saw the grieving mother and He told her not to cry. The pallbearers stopped as He touched the funeral bier (*open coffin*). Jesus said, "Young man, I say to you 'Arise'". The dead man awoke from the sleep of death. He sat up and spoke, and Jesus gave him back to his mother.

Everyone in the crowd was awe-struck. A reverent fear seized them all as they praised God and gave Him thanks. They said a great Prophet had appeared to them and God had visited His people. The good news quickly spread throughout all Judea.

There are many today who are dead in their sins. Jesus only needs an invitation to come into our life so He can raise us from a spiritual death. He forgives when we repent and follow His commands including confession that He is the Son of God and are baptized for the cancellation (*remission*) of our sins (*Acts 2:38*).

Are You the Coming One? (Luke 7:18-35)

John the Baptist was in prison when he heard about Jesus' miracles of raising the widow's son from the dead and healing the centurion's servant. John sent two of his disciples to Jesus to ask Him, "Are You the Coming One, or do we look for another?" This was and still is a very important question, for it has an eternal impact on many souls. John needed to know if Christ was the Messiah that had been prophesied for centuries. If not, they would look for the future coming of the Messiah.

At the time this question was posed to Christ, He was very busy healing many who were ill, distressed with body plagues and evil spirits, and many blind folks. His work was never done, for there were so many in need of His healing or cleansing touch.

Jesus told John the Baptist's disciples to go and tell him what they had witnessed and heard: the blind, the deaf, the lame, and the lepers had all been healed in their presence. People were raised from the dead, and the poor had heard the good news (*Gospel*) preached to them. This fulfilled the Scriptures in Isaiah 29:18-19, 35:5-6, and 61:1.

Jesus said that regardless of our outward circumstances, we can be blessed and happy because of God's favor and salvation. He said further that if anyone does not take offense in Him, we will find happiness and blessings. John's disciples left Jesus to give His report to John.

Jesus then asked His disciples what they went to see in the desert. Was it a reed shaken by the wind, a man dressed in soft garments, or a prophet? He told them the men dressed in fine apparel sat in luxury in courts or palaces. Jesus then quoted Malachi 3:1 about John the Baptist and Himself: "Behold, I will send my messenger; and he shall prepare the way before me: and the Lord, whom ye seek, shall suddenly come to his temple, even the messenger of the covenant, whom ye delight in: behold, he shall come, saith the LORD of hosts." Jesus said John the Baptist was a great prophet, but the least person in the kingdom of God is even greater.

Many people heard these words from Jesus and acknowledged the justice of God in calling them to repentance and the baptism of John the Baptist. As usual, the Pharisees and lawyers of the Mosaic Law rejected God's purpose by refusing Jesus' message. Jesus compared these obstinate disbelievers to little children who played music in the marketplace and were ignored as no one danced or wept. In short, Jesus was saying the disbelievers were totally insensitive to the good news of the Gospel; they heard it but failed to act. His message with eternal value was a non-event to the disbelievers.

They called John the Baptist a demon because of his very unusual diet of locusts and honey. Then Jesus came and ate a regular diet, and they called Him a glutton and wine drinker, a friend of tax collectors, and well-known sinners. Believers prove the wisdom of God is true and divine by their actions and character, while disbelievers discredit and deny the power of God.

Jesus then accepted an invitation to go home with a Pharisee to share a meal. There was a very sinful woman who lived in town. She heard Jesus was eating with the Pharisee, so she brought a flask of fragrant perfume. She stood behind Jesus and began weeping. Her tears fell to Jesus' feet and she wiped His feet with her hair. The sinful woman affectionately kissed Jesus' feet and anointed them with her perfume. Jesus did not try and shield Himself from the sinful woman who was a social outcast. Her devotion to sin was transformed into love and adoration for Christ.

Jesus wanted to give His host something to consider through a parable. He said a lender of money had two debtors. One owed him five hundred denarii and the other owed fifty. Neither borrower had money to pay the lender, so he forgave the debt of each debtor. Jesus' question was: "Which of them will love the lender more?" Simon felt the man who owed the most would love the lender more and Jesus agreed.

Jesus then told Simon who witnessed the sinful woman's kind deeds something very troubling. When Jesus entered Simon's house, Simon did not give Jesus any water to wash His feet as was the custom. Jesus told Simon neither did he kiss His feet, but the woman used her tears, her hair, and her expensive perfume to anoint His feet. The one who loves Jesus a little will be forgiven little. Jesus pronounced forgiveness to the woman for her sins. She had shown love and compassion and He tenderly forgave her of her many sins. He told the woman to go in peace because her faith had saved her. She no longer needed to be stressed over the consequences of sin; for Jesus had lifted that burden.

Luke 7 reveals Jesus' power over illness, death, and sin. He is all-powerful over any problem we encounter. We need to have the centurion's faith to fully believe in His power without even seeing Him.

Women's Role (Luke 8:1-3)

Women have always played an important role in the religious world. Many great women such as Sarah, Ruth, Naomi, Lydia, Elizabeth, Mary, and others are mentioned prominently in the Scriptures.

There was a sizable group of women who supported Jesus and His disciples in their ministry. These women served Jesus faithfully so they could make His mission a little easier. It is interesting that one of the women had a shady and sinful background, but her life was changed when she met Christ. The women were devoted and loyal to this group of men who changed the religious world for all time.

One of the women was Mary Magdalene who was demon-possessed as Satan had full control of her life. Jesus cast seven demons out of Mary Magdalene so she could regain her life and live for Christ. She became a special woman in the work of the Lord.

- In Luke 8:2, she received salvation.
- In Mark 15:40-41, she showed gratitude through her faithful ministry for Christ.
- In John 19:25, she was at the cross when Jesus died.
- In John 20:11-18, she wept outside Jesus' tomb as she tried to find Him.

God can take a person who has wasted their life on sin and turn them into a useful vessel for His kingdom work. These women provided for Jesus' needs by sharing their physical resources with Him.

Women are still an important part of the Lord's work today. They give what they have through their service including missions outreach, praying, witnessing, worship, etc. The church would be weakened tremendously without the care and compassion that is best shown by women.

In Luke 8, Jesus taught three parables and He demonstrated His God-given power once again:

Parable of the Sower (Luke 8:15)

In Jesus' day, a farmer would till his soil and broadcast the seed by hand. Some fields often had a combination of packed soil like a pathway, rocky spots, thorn patches, and good fertile soil. A man went out to sow a crop of grain. As he broadcast the seed, some fell on the good and bad soil. The seed that fell on the packed pathway was quickly eaten by the birds. The seed on the rocky spots sprouted, but quickly withered because it did not have moisture. The seed in the thorn patches grew, but the thorns choked it out. Only the seed that fell on good soil yielded a crop a hundred-fold. The different types of soil represent the hearts of man. Some hearts are hardened due to sin, some are too busy with earthly cares, but some are open and receptive to the Word of God.

Jesus called on the people receiving this parable to hear, listen, ponder, and understand His teaching. They needed to know how to apply His teaching to their lives, so Jesus proceeded to tell them what the parable meant. He wanted them to recognize very clearly the mysteries and secrets of the kingdom of God. Jesus knew some would hear and see, but not comprehend His teaching.

The meaning of the parable is quite simple. The seed is the Word of God.

- The hearers on the packed pathway heard the message, but the devil robbed the message from their hearts like a flock of birds. Without retaining the message of Christ they would fail to be saved for eternity.
- The seed that fell on the rocky spots represent the people who joyfully hear, receive, and welcome the Word, but the truth does not take root in their hearts. They believe the message until trials come,

and they quickly forfeit what they heard about Christ.

- The seed in the thorny patches are people who hear, but the cares of this life overwhelm them. Anxiety, stress, riches, and pleasures causes their fruit to not ripen. The Word therefore cannot be perfected in their lives.
- The seed on the good soil are the ones who hear the Word, hold it fast in a thankful heart, and constantly and patiently bear fruit for the Lord. These are the people who are committed to endure to the end.

Our lives reflect what type of heart we have for the Lord's message. Some are hard-hearted, so they continue serving Satan. Others will gladly receive the Word but fail to cling to it in times of trial and temptation. Some will hear and know the truth, but they let cares and pleasures rob them of their relationship with the Lord. The truly loyal and dedicated believer will joyfully receive the Word, apply it to their lives, and bear much fruit for the Lord. They are willing to patiently endure the disappointments of life and stay focused on the Lord regardless of their circumstances.

We may be living for Satan and represent the packed soil. Satan has hardened our hearts making it difficult for the truth of God to penetrate our lives. Christ came so our lives can be changed into productive servants for Him. We learn patient endurance in Christ when we accept Him.

Jesus taught another very short lesson on the power of light in Luke 8:16-18. No one lights a lamp and covers it so the light is blocked from giving visibility. Christians are to openly display the light of the truth of the Gospel by telling others who do not believe. We share what Christ means to us so they too can know the Lord. We point them to Christ who can change their life and lift the burden of sin. By openly revealing Christ, we show others the value and joy in serving Jesus. Our lives are to be like mirrors that reflect the love and forgiveness of our Lord. Jesus warns us to be careful how we listen. Those who have spiritual knowledge will increase their knowledge of the Lord, but those who have a little spiritual knowledge can lose what they have as it can be taken away.

Jesus' Power Over Nature (Luke 8:22-25)

Jesus and the Holy Spirit were present with God when the heavens and the earth were created. God said in Genesis1:26, "Let us make man in Our image, according to Our likeness." John 1:2 tells us, "He (*Christ*) was in the beginning with God." Christ and the Holy Spirit are eternal just like God. These verses clearly establish the deity and divinity of Christ.

One day, Jesus got in a boat with His disciples to sail to the other side of the sea. During the voyage Jesus fell to sleep. A twisting whirlwind set down on the water and the boat began filling with water. They were in danger of sinking so the disciples awoke Jesus and told him they were about to perish. Jesus got up and rebuked the wind and raging waves, and they instantly calmed when He said, "Peace, be still."

Jesus asked the disciples why they were so fearful. He wanted to know what happened to their faith in Him during the wind storm. A reverential and awesome fear fell on the disciples as they asked who Jesus was, that He commanded even the wind and waves to obey Him. They were eye-witnesses to the power of God being carried out by His Son.

Jesus' Power Over Demons (Luke 8:26-38)

Jesus not only had power over nature, but he also had ultimate power over Satan and his demons or angels. Jesus and the disciples got to the other side of the sea. He stepped out of the boat and met a demon-possessed man. This man was insane due to the demons that lived within. He wore no clothes, and he lived in the cemetery. The demons were so powerful that they would bind the man with chains, but he was so strong he would break them. The demons completely ruled this man's life in an awful manner.

The man fell down before Jesus and cried out in terror, "What have I to do with thee, Jesus, thou Son of God most high? I beseech thee, torment me not." Jesus asked the man his name and he said, "Legion," because many devils were living in his body. A legion in Roman terms meant one thousand, but it could represent up to five thousand. There were many demons in this man.

The demons begged Jesus to not send them into the bottomless pit of hell. A herd of hogs was nearby on the mountain, and the demons implored Jesus to send them out of the demoniac man into the swine. Jesus cast the demons out of the man and into the hogs. The swine ran violently down the mountain and into the sea where they drowned.

Some of the eye-witnesses to this powerful event went into the city to tell what Jesus did. The people came out and found the freed man sitting fully clothed at Jesus' feet. The people were afraid when they saw the man in his right mind. They saw how this previously insane man had been healed. The people should have been ecstatic over what Jesus did, but instead they were fearful and asked the freed man to leave. He wanted to go with Jesus, but He gave the man a greater mission. Jesus told him to go home and witness how God had done such a great thing for him. Our families can be our best mission field.

<u>Jesus' Power Over Disease and Death</u> (Luke 8:40-56)

Jesus returned to Galilee and the crowd received and welcomed Him with gladness and joy. They had been waiting on and looking for His return. Jesus met Jairus who had been a director in the synagogue for a long time. He fell at Jesus' feet and begged Him to come to his house. His only daughter who was about twelve years old was dying. Jesus went with a press of people crowding around Him. There was such a crowd that they almost suffocated Jesus.

A woman was in the crowd and she had been hemorrhaging blood for twelve years. She had spent all she had going from one physician to another, but they had been unable to help her. She must have been very weak from losing such a large amount of blood. She was desperate for Jesus' healing touch. She was in the crowd behind Jesus and touched the hem of His garment. Immediately her flow of blood stopped.

Jesus asked who touched Him for He felt healing power leave His body. The woman came in front of Jesus and fell trembling before Him. She told Him she had touched His garment and was cured instantly. Jesus compassionately told the woman, "Daughter, be of good comfort: thy faith hath made thee whole; go in peace." Out of desperation, she found Jesus, and He healed her completely.

Jesus still intended to go to Jairus' house where his daughter was critically ill. A man from Jairus' house came to announce that his daughter had died and there was no need to bother Jesus further. Jesus told the man to not be alarmed or afraid, but simply believe in His power so the girl could be brought back to life. Jesus arrived at the house and told the crowd to stay outside. He only permitted Peter, James, John, and the parents to go inside with Him. Jesus told the people who were weeping outside to not mourn for the girl was not dead but sleeping. They laughed at Jesus and scorned Him for such a ridiculous statement, for they knew with certainty she was dead.

Jesus took the little girl's hand and commanded her to arise from her sleep of death. She started breathing and got up immediately. Jesus told her parents to give their daughter something to eat. Her parents were amazed, but Jesus commanded them to tell no one what had happened. We don't know why Jesus did not want the good news shared with the others who were so sad.

The summary of this chapter:

- Women are very important in ministry support
- The condition of our heart determines our receptivity to the truth of the Gospel
- Every believer is to be a shining light in the dark world of sin
- Jesus still has power over Satan, illness, the forces of nature, and even death.

Our full commitment to the Lord is needed if we are to excel in His kingdom work.

Chapter Six
The Great Confession

Sending Out the Apostles (Luke 9:1-5)

After Judas Iscariot betrayed Christ, he committed suicide as he obviously had lost all hope as one of Jesus' original twelve disciples. This left a vacancy that needed to be filled. In Acts 1:26, Matthias was chosen to replace Judas Iscariot. In Luke 9:1, Jesus commissioned these twelve men to go out and change the religious world. They were not qualified to do this important work for God, but Jesus gave them power and authority over all demons and diseases. In Acts 1:8, Jesus told His apostles, "But ye shall receive power, after that the Holy Ghost is come upon you: and ye shall be witnesses unto me both in Jerusalem, and in all Judea, and in Samaria, and unto the uttermost part of the earth." Jesus still has the ability to empower us through the Holy Spirit to do unbelievable work.

When Saul was converted from Judaism in Damascus, Jesus told Ananias in Acts 9:15 that

Saul would become a chosen vessel to preach His name to the Gentiles, kings, and the children of Israel. Saul had been a persecutor of Christians, but Jesus would commission him to be a preacher to make more Christians. His name was changed to Paul and in 2 Corinthians 2:1, he said he was an apostle of Jesus Christ by the will of God. God intended for Paul to be an apostle (*one who is sent*) to spread the good news of the Gospel.

These men were sent into Asia Minor to preach, teach, baptize, and heal the sick. Jesus gave them explicit instructions to not take anything for their personal use including a staff for walking, a bag with clothing and personal items, food, or money. They were to only wear one tunic (*outer garment*).

The apostles were to visit homes and spend the night. If a family rejected them, Christ told them to leave and shake the dust from their feet as a testimony they had been rejected. The apostles were not embarking on a pleasure trip as they would need to rely fully on God to lead them to families who could meet their daily needs, and also be receptive to their message. They followed the Lord's instructions and started visiting towns so they could preach, baptize, and heal.

Herod (Luke 9:7-9)

False rumors were circulating that John, who had been executed, had risen from the dead. Herod had ordered the beheading of John. Another rumor was that Elijah, the prophet who had been dead for many years, had risen from the dead. Herod was a tetrarch in the Roman government. Tetrarch in Greek meant ruler of a quarter (*a province or region*). Herod was aware of the rumors and was confused due to the conflicting rumors. He wanted to see John or Elijah, whichever had risen from the dead. Herod wanted this person who had come forth from death to show him proof that they were truly resurrected.

Feeding Five Thousand Men (Luke 9:10-17)

Parallel Scriptures to the account recorded in Luke of Jesus feeding the multitude are found in Matthew 14:13-21, Mark 6:32-44, and John 6:5-23.

Jesus and His disciples had retreated to Bethsaida near the Sea of Galilee, but the crowds found them and followed Jesus. Bethsaida was the birth place of Peter, Andrew, and Phillip. Jesus welcomed the many disciples who had come. He taught them about the kingdom of God and healed all those with illnesses. Moses and Elisha had fed God's children in the desert many years ago, and now Jesus, their Messiah would feed the crowd on a mountainside outside Jerusalem.

It was afternoon when the disciples came to Jesus to ask Him to send the crowd of about five thousand men (*plus women and children*) away so they could find food and lodging. There were likely fifteen to twenty thousand people including the women and children in the crowd. Jesus told the disciples to give them something to eat. They told Jesus they could only find five small loaves of bread and two fish in the entire crowd. Jesus told the disciples to have the people sit in groups of about fifty each.

Jesus looked up into heaven and pronounced His blessings on the meager meal. He gave the multiplied food to the disciples to distribute to the crowd. Every person ate until they were filled, and the disciples then gathered up twelve baskets of left-over bread. When Jesus blesses, we can expect abundance beyond our need.

Peter's Great Confession (Luke 9:18-27)

After feeding the crowd, Jesus went to be alone so He could pray. This one-on-one time with God empowered Christ to perform miracles and reveal the will of God to man. The disciples then joined Christ, and He asked them an important question: "Who do the crowds say that I am" (Luke 9:18)? Jesus wanted to know if His message as their Messiah was being accepted by the people. He came from heaven to earth to be our Savior, but many had rejected His origin and His message.

The disciples told Jesus some thought He was John the Baptist, Elias, or one of the old prophets who had risen from the dead. Jesus then asked, "But who say ye that I am?" (Luke 9:20) Peter quickly answered, "Thou art the Christ, the Son of the living God." Peter's great confession became the bedrock upon which the church has been built. Christ is the sure foundation for every Christian and every God-fearing church that is carrying out Christ's mission of salvation for the lost.

Jesus told the disciples He would suffer many things, and be rejected by elders, chief priests, and scribes. His final earthly destination would be the cross so His blood could be shed to cleanse us from sin. The good news is that He would arise from the dead on the third day after His crucifixion.

Our salvation cost Christ His earthly life before God gave Him a glorified body that will never die. Likewise, our salvation comes with a price attached. He said when we accept Him we must deny self, take up our cross, and follow Him daily. Being a Christ-follower is a daily opportunity to suffer for His sake as we witness to others who do not know Him. If we selfishly keep our knowledge of Christ to ourselves, our friends may die in their sins without ever knowing Christ. Many suffer persecution because of their faith in God. Jesus promises heavenly restoration of an earthly life surrendered in His work.

Jesus then issued a warning and told the disciples not to tell anyone what He was getting ready to reveal to them. He said He would suffer many things and be rejected by many. The religious elite including the elders, chief priests, and scribes would have Him killed; but Jesus gave them the good news of His pending resurrection from death on the third day after He would be crucified.

<u>The Cost of Following Jesus</u> (Luke 9:23-27, Luke 9:57-62)

All things of any value cost something. The cost of things we consume daily (*food, fuel, rent, medicine, etc.*) has risen sharply in recent months. This places people with low or fixed incomes in a very precarious position. We must decide which goods or services we can eliminate to be able to buy the absolute necessities. Some may even be faced with rationing so they can survive.

Our salvation cost Christ His earthly life when He died on the cross so His shed blood can wash away our sins. He could not have given more, as He gave His all. It was out of His extreme love for every lost person and His tenacious desire to do His Father's will that He went to the cross.

It has been said that freedom is not free due to the innocent lives lost in battle around the globe.

Neither is our salvation free as it took Christ's death so we can have a loving relationship with God and the promise of eternal life with Him. Jesus' first requirement of every follower is that we must deny self so we can take up our personal cross daily to follow Him. This means if we are a prideful and proud person, we must get over ourselves so we can follow Christ.

Jesus said if we try to save this life we will lose it, but we can be saved if we are willing to lose this life for His sake. We are to surrender our personal ambitions and goals and give Christ full reign in our lives. It is a drastic change in our daily life to surrender our all to Jesus. We imitate Christ when we surrender our will to Him, just as He surrendered His will to the Father prior to His crucifixion. Because He was resurrected, we gain spiritual blessings through surrender.

Jesus also warns us that if we are ashamed of Him and His words, then He will be ashamed of us before God when He returns to rapture His church. He will come back with the holy angels in glory and magnificence. Jesus was certainly not ashamed to be stripped and beaten for us, so we cannot afford to be ashamed of Him. We can never praise Him enough for His supreme sacrifice on our behalf.

Jesus said some who are living when He returns will not taste an earthly death. They will be alive when Jesus steps out on the clouds to call His redeemed children home. Those whose bodies are asleep in Jesus will be raised to receive their glorified bodies that will never die again. The believers who are living when Jesus comes back will rise with the resurrected saints to meet the Lord in the air. (1 Thessalonians 4:17)

Jesus continued His discourse on the cost of discipleship in Luke 9:57-62. One of the disciples told Jesus he would follow Him wherever He went. Jesus reminded the disciples that foxes have holes and birds have nests, but He did not have a place to lay His head.

Some make excuses for shying away from serving Christ fully. One man told Jesus that he had to first go and bury his father. He was going to wait on his father to die before following Christ. Jesus told the man to let the dead bury their own dead, but this man should go abroad to publish the good news about the kingdom of God.

Another man had bought a piece of ground and needed to go see it, so he asked to be excused by Jesus. One man said he had just married and could not come to follow Him. Another man told Jesus he would follow Him and become His disciple, but he needed to first tell his loved ones good-bye. Jesus replied that no one who puts his hand to the plow and looks back to the things behind is fit for the kingdom of God. Serving Christ is a commitment for today and the days ahead. Excuses for not following Christ are not an option.

Jesus is Transfigured (Luke 9:28-36)

Eight days later Jesus took Peter, James, and John, His inner-circle of disciples, to the mountain to pray. As Jesus prayed, the appearance of His face changed and His robe became glistening white. Moses and Elijah, who had died centuries previously, came from heaven to visit Jesus on the mountain that day. They too had a heavenly glow as they talked to Jesus about His upcoming departure from earth. God would soon deliver Jesus from the problems of this earth as He must die, rise from the dead, and ascend back to the Father in heaven.

Peter, James, and John fell into a deep sleep while the conversation took place between Moses, Elijah, and Jesus. Then they awoke and saw this glorious trio together. They had slept through the conversation between Moses, Elijah, and Jesus. Moses and Elijah were ready to depart when Peter asked Jesus if they could build three tabernacles (*huts*) in honor to Moses, Elijah, and Jesus. Peter thought he had a good idea, but he was still ignorant about Jesus' upcoming destiny at the cross.

God sent a cloud and Peter, James, and John were afraid of what was happening. They had never experienced anything like this before. God's voice came out of the cloud that said, "This is my beloved Son, hear Him." The disciples were to tell no one of what they had seen in the transfiguration.

Jesus and His three closest disciples spent the night on the mountain. Peter, James, and John must have been overwhelmed when they saw Moses and Elijah come to the mountain from heaven. This was an experience they would never forget. The afterglow of excitement, peace, and amazement would linger with them in future days.

Jesus' Power Over Demons (Luke 9:37-42)

The four men came off the mountain the next morning where a large crowd met them. They had no idea what had transpired on the mountain when Moses and Elijah appeared. A man was in the crowd and he called out to Jesus about his only son who had a severe problem. An evil spirit possessed the lad and it would throw him on the ground as he screamed and foamed at the mouth. The spirit was completely destroying the young boy. The man had asked Jesus' other disciples to drive the spirit out, but they did not have the power to deal with it.

Jesus told the disciples and the crowd they did not believe and they were a perverse (*wayward*) generation. He asked the people how long they thought He would be with them. Jesus told the father to bring his son to Him. While the man was bringing his son to Jesus, the demon threw him down and he had convulsions. Jesus rebuked the evil spirit, healed the child, and gave him to his father.

Everyone was amazed when they witnessed the evidence of God's power working through Jesus. While the people talked with excitement, Jesus told His disciples to let His words sink into their ears and minds. He told them the Son of Man was about to be delivered into the hands of ungodly men. The disciples failed to grasp what Jesus was telling them. They did not understand what Jesus was saying, but they were afraid to ask for a further explanation.

The Controversy (Luke 9:46-50)

A silly dispute erupted among the disciples as they asked Jesus a very selfish question. They wanted to know which of the disciples was the greatest in Jesus' eyes. Who would have the most authority and be more worthy? Jesus used a little child to set them straight. There was no room for bickering among His disciples. He set the child by His side and told the disciples that whoever accepted the child in His name and for His sake would also receive and welcome Him. Then He said that whoever accepted Him also accepted His Father who sent Him. He said the one among them who was the least would be the greatest. This very brief lesson on humility is still very important today as we serve alongside others in God's kingdom work. We are equal in God's sight, so the position we hold does not elevate us above others who also strive to do God's work. The person in the pew is just as important as the person in the pulpit, as God loves each of us equally.

John told Jesus they had witnessed a man casting out demons in His name, but they ordered him to stop because he did not follow them. Jesus told John that he should not forbid anyone who was not against them as he was doing the right thing. We do not have the privilege or obligation to restrict anyone from doing God's work as long as they are sincerely trying to follow the Lord's command to love their neighbor.

Rejection (Luke 9:51-56)

Although Jesus performed one miracle after another, men still chose to reject Him. Worshiping Jesus was totally different than the Old Testament worship in the synagogue or temple. Some readily embraced Jesus and His message while others openly rejected Him.

The time of Jesus' crucifixion, resurrection, and ascension back to heaven was quickly approaching. Jesus decided to go back to Jerusalem where the annual Passover Feast would be held. Some of Jesus' followers went ahead of Him as He started His journey. The messengers stopped in a Samaritan village that was normally off-limits for the Jews. The men were to prepare for Jesus' arrival, but the Samaritans rejected His visit. They had the opportunity to be visited by the Son of God, but they refused to accept Him into their village.

James and John witnessed this rejection, so they asked Jesus if He wanted them to order fire to come down from heaven and consume them, even as Elijah did in 2 Kings 1:9-16. Jesus rebuked them and said they didn't know the kind of spirit they had that gave them this thought. He told them He did not come to destroy men, but to save them from the penalty of sin. They continued their journey to another village.

Men still reject Christ today, even after learning of His saving grace and forgiveness. Our prayer must be for God to open their eyes to the salvation He offers that will result in eternal life with Him.

Chapter Seven
Judgment and Rejoicing

The Bible teaches us about God's judgment and how we find cause to rejoice as His child. Judgment can be good or bad. If a judge in a courtroom finds the defendant innocent, then there is rejoicing because they have retained their freedom. However, if the defendant is found guilty, he/she must pay for their crime through fines, imprisonment, probation, community service, etc. Luke 10 covers the topics of judgment on unrepentant cities and rejoicing over the blessing of service to the Lord.

Seventy Sent Out (Luke 10:1-12 & Luke 10:17-20)

Jesus appointed seventy disciples that were in addition to the initial twelve disciples he called. He sent these seventy disciples in pairs into every city where He was preparing to go. He told them there was an abundant crop (*of unbelievers*), but there were far too few to go witness to them. Jesus used the analogy of a farmer with an abundant crop with too few laborers to bring in the harvest. Jesus sent the thirty-five teams out like lambs into a pack of hungry wild wolves.

Jesus instructed these men to not take any personal belongings with them. They were to take no money, no personal clothing, and no change of sandals. They went in faith they would be well-received and cared for by perfect strangers. They were to keep moving and not stop to visit along the way. When they entered a house, they were to pronounce peace upon it, hoping the host would appreciate their freedom from sin and stress. Some would receive the blessing of the disciples, but unbelievers would reject them as their guests.

If the host was hospitable, they were to stay indefinitely, and eat the food and drink the family provided. Jesus instructed them to not move from house to house. They were to heal the sick and let them know the kingdom of God had come near to them. If the town rejected them they were to go into the streets and wipe the dust off their feet. This action would be a testimony against those who did not believe and rejected them. They were to let the unbelievers know the kingdom of God had come close to them, but they had rejected the peace that comes from knowing

God. Jesus said in the Last Day Sodom, that was destroyed with fire and brimstone (*burning sulphur*), would be in better shape than any town or home that rejected these disciples.

In Luke 10:17-20, the seventy disciples returned home proclaiming with delight and joy that even the demons were subject to them when they drove them out in Jesus' name. Jesus told them He saw Satan falling like a lightning flash from heaven. These men were given great power and authority over Satan and his demons. They could trample serpents and scorpions and not be harmed. They could overcome anything Satan threw at them without any harm befalling them.

Jesus told them to not rejoice over the power He gave them, but to rejoice in the fact their names were written in the Lamb's book of life. No matter what we possess, how much leadership ability we may have, or our accomplishments, nothing is more important than having our names written in the book of life in heaven. The things of this life cannot compare to what Jesus has in store for every one of His children.

<u>Judgment on Wicked Cities</u> (Luke 10:13-16)

Jesus called out certain cities by name when He pronounced judgment upon them. He said His judgment would come to Chorazin, Bethsaida, Tyre, Sidon, and Capernaum. Many of the hard-hearted citizens in these cities had obviously misused their privileges. They refused to repent of their short-comings. Jesus told them they would be brought down because they had rejected Him. When man rejects Christ, they also reject the God who sent Him to earth as our Savior.

The Bible warns us about death and judgment. Hebrews 9:27 tells us it is appointed unto man to die an earthly death, and after this the judgment (*of God*). We cannot delay or cancel this appointment as it has been set by God. Death is one of the most certain things of life. Both the young and old die every day.

It is recorded in Jude 1:14-15, the Lord will come back with His saints who died an earthly death to execute judgment on the godly and the ungodly. He will show unrepentant sinners their ungodly words, deeds, and actions. There is a day of accountability in the future; we may dismiss or deny it, but this is a part of God's plan that we cannot change.

In Revelation 20:12, the Apostle John wrote, "And I saw the dead, small and great, stand before God; and the books were opened; and another book was opened, which is the book of life; and the dead were judged out of those things which were written in the books, according to their works."

Jesus' Joy (Luke 10:21-24)

God has revealed His plan of salvation to all who will believe regardless of our educational level. We don't need a university degree to understand God's plan of love and forgiveness for all who will come in repentance for their sins.

John 3:16-17 says, "For God so loved the world that He gave His only begotten Son, that whosoever believeth in him should not perish, but have everlasting life. For God sent not his Son into the world to condemn the world; but that the world through him might be saved." Every person regardless of their economic or educational status can come in faith believing, and confessing Jesus is the Son of God and be saved from their sins. God sent Jesus out of love to save and not to condemn.

This gives us reason to rejoice that God loved us so much that He was willing to let Jesus be our sacrificial Lamb to die on the cross. His blood cleanses us from all sin when we repent and confess Him.

Jesus said these secret things regarding salvation were revealed to Him by His Father who sent Him from heaven to earth. Jesus told His disciples about the secret to forgiveness and joy so they in turn could tell others. Many prophets and kings in Jesus' day would have liked to have seen and heard the words Jesus spoke to His disciples. The secrets of salvation have now been fully revealed through the Bible to every person who wants to come to Christ. Salvation is available to all without exception.

The Good Samaritan (Luke 10:25-37)

A lawyer asked Jesus what he needed to do to inherit everlasting life in the Messiah's kingdom. This is a legitimate question from any person. This man was well educated in the legal field, but he wanted to learn what he needed to do to live in eternity with Christ. His heart was right when he asked the question.

Jesus asked the lawyer what was written in the Law (*of Moses*). The lawyer answered that we must love the Lord our God with all our heart, soul, strength, and mind; and love our neighbor as much as we love self. He knew the Law when he quoted from Leviticus 19:18 and Deuteronomy 6:5. Jesus told him he had given the correct answer, and he must do these things to inherit eternal life. Then the lawyer asked Jesus a very important question, "And who is my neighbor?" This question led Jesus to teach a very important lesson through a parable *(a physical earthly story with a heavenly spiritual meaning)*.

A man was traveling from Jerusalem down to Jericho when he was attacked by highway robbers. They took his clothes and personal belongings and beat him unmercifully. They left the half-dead man lying on the side of the road. The robbers didn't care if the man lived or died.

A priest came down the road and saw the suffering man but crossed the road as he did not want to get involved. Then a Levite came and saw him and he too crossed the road. He did not want to run the risk of becoming ceremonially unclean by touching a dying man. A Samaritan, who was a heathen in the Jews' eyes, came to the injured man. He had pity and sympathy for him, so he cleaned and dressed his wounds. The Samaritan put the man on his animal and took him to an inn for further care. He gave the innkeeper two day's wages to take care of the man, and he told the innkeeper he would come back and pay him more if needed.

Jesus asked the lawyer which of these three proved to be a neighbor to this victim of robbers. The lawyer said the one who showed pity and mercy was a true neighbor. Jesus told the lawyer to go and do likewise.

This lesson on pity and compassion extends from the lawyer to every believer today. We sometimes close our eyes to obvious opportunities to serve our fellow man. We can be like the priest or the Levite and not want to get involved. A laborer in Christ's kingdom must be willing to get their hands dirty at times to be of service to others. This takes humility, compassion, pity, and sympathy to serve to the fullest. We need to demonstrate the sacrificial love of the Samaritan as we serve Christ and others.

The Women's Service (Luke 10:38-42)

Jesus visited two sisters, Mary and Martha, in their home. They welcomed Jesus into their home as He had visited them on several occasions. Mary sat at Jesus' feet as He taught while Martha was busy preparing a meal. Martha was on a mission to feed Jesus so she was temporarily distracted from His teaching. Martha asked Jesus if it did not matter to Him that Mary had left her alone to prepare the meal. She asked Jesus to instruct Mary to help get the food ready. Jesus responded to Martha in Luke 10:41-42, "Martha, Martha, thou are careful and troubled about many things: but one thing is needful; and Mary hath chosen that good part, which shall not be taken away from her." Instead of criticizing Mary, Jesus commended her for her devotion to Him.

There are many distractions that can cause us to forget the important things in serving Christ. The problems of pride and greed may cause us to focus more on self than Christ. We must be careful to keep our activities and behavior in proper perspective and balance as we strive to serve Christ, our families, and others. Being too busy for the Lord can be detrimental in our relationship with Him.

A motto used in a Christian youth camp many years ago said, "Christ first, others second, and self third."

Chapter Eight
Prayer and Seeking

When we pray, we are seeking guidance from God through the Holy Spirit. The Holy Spirit comes into our lives to dwell once we accept Christ as our Lord and are immersed into Him. (Acts 2:38) God works through the Holy Spirit to lead, guide, instruct, convict, and encourage us in our Christian journey. Seeking and praying go hand-in-hand as we strive to live more righteous and holy lives. Our prayer life is critical in having a proper relationship with God and His Son. Jesus felt a need to regularly steal away from the crowd so He could be alone with God and pray. He sought God's power for miracles and guidance for His ministry. He set the example for our prayer life when He gave us His model prayer.

The Lord's Prayer (Matthew 6:1-13)

Jesus warns us to not be hypocritical when we pray. We do not pray to be seen or heard by man as our prayer is a personal talk with God. A good deed for others is to also be done in secret without expecting a return. God will reward us openly for our good deeds on the Last Day. (Matthew 6:4)

Jesus encourages and instructs us to pray in private without any outside influence. We are to pour our hearts out in sincerity to God without trying to use fancy words and phrases. After all, God knows the things we need before we even ask. God expects humility, not eloquence, when we pray.

Matthew's record of the Lord's Prayer is more complete than what Luke wrote in Luke 11. Jesus first acknowledged God as our Father in heaven, and He says how hallowed (*holy*) God is. Jesus asked God for His kingdom to come, and for His will to be done on earth as it is in heaven. He then asked God for His daily provision of food. He sought God's forgiveness of our sin debt just like we forgive others. Human forgiveness shows God and others sincere repentance for our sins. When we forgive, all resentment is to depart. God's forgiveness is conditional based on our willingness to forgive others. Jesus knew we need deliverance from temptation, so He asked God for His help with Satan. He closes His prayer by acknowledging God's kingdom, power, and glory forever. When Jesus closed His prayer with the word, "Amen," He was asking God to let it be so.

Christians are given the liberty to pray as we are led by the Holy Spirit. We can utter the same words Jesus prayed in His model prayer, or we can craft a prayer based on the thoughts and intents of our heart. When we look closely at how Jesus prayed, we see God in charge of everything. He is our all-powerful Creator as He sustains His kingdom. God is holy and righteous while we are frail with a sinful nature. He has a kingdom that will come with Jesus when He raptures His church. His kingdom will be our eternal home after this life. God provides all our needs, and He forgives sin when we repent. We are to be just as forgiving as God when others do harm to us. Jesus recognized Satan's power over man, so He sought God's strength to overcome.

Asking and Receiving (Luke 11:5-13)

Jesus then gave His disciples a brief lesson about friendship and perseverance. He said a man was in bed with his children. A friend knocked on his door at midnight asking for three loaves of bread for an unexpected visitor. The man told his neighbor he could not give him any bread as his door was shut. The neighbor persisted in his request, so the man finally got up and gave him the loaves he needed.

Sometimes we have the resources and ability to answer God's call, but the call comes at a very inconvenient time; so we initially decline the request. The person may persist in asking for our help, and we finally give in. In answering the call, we receive more blessings than expected. God's work is very important, and it is up to each of us to answer the call to rise and work. We can be the persistent one asking for help or the reluctant one who delays to respond to the call. Persistence and perseverance are both needed in God's kingdom work.

One of Jesus' most memorable and prominent statements for the Christian is found in Luke 11:9, "Ask, and it shall be given you; seek, and ye shall find; knock, and it shall be opened unto you." This command is also recorded in Matthew 7:7, John 15:7, and 1 John 3:22. We are to abide in Christ if we want to be able to ask, seek, and find an answer to our requests.

Jesus promises that if we ask we will receive; seek and we will find; knock and the door of opportunity will open. Jesus has the key to every door that represents obstacles on life's pathway. He said if our child asks for bread, would we give him a stone instead? If the child asks for a fish or an egg, would we give him a serpent or scorpion? The obvious answer is that a loving father will do everything in his power to meet his child's needs without offering fake or harmful substitutes. Jesus then drove the point home by saying if we know how to give good gifts, how much more will our heavenly Father give the Holy Spirit to those who ask?

A House Divided (Luke 11:14:23)

Jesus encountered a dumb person who could not speak because he was possessed by the devil. Jesus cast out the demon and the person started speaking normally. The witnesses to this miracle thought Jesus had cast out demons by Beelzebub, the chief ruler of all demons. Jesus saw a division among the people because some wanted a sign from heaven as they tried to figure out who Jesus was and on what authority He performed this miracle.

Jesus told them that a divided kingdom is brought to desolation, and a house divided is going to fall. Satan is divided and far from God. One day Satan will fall when he is cast into the lake of fire in the end time (Revelation 19:20). Jesus cast out demons with the help of God; so God's kingdom had come upon those listening to Him. He said in Luke 11:23, "He that is not with me is against me." It is very clear: we must be constantly connected to and in agreement with Christ so our spiritual house is not divided.

John 12:25 tells us, "He that loveth his life shall lose it; he that hateth his life in this world shall keep it unto life eternal." Judson Van de Venter and Winfield Weeden said in a vintage hymn, "All to Jesus I surrender, all to Him I freely give; I will ever love and trust Him, in His presence daily live." What a privilege we are given to be able to surrender our will and walk with the Lord each day.

The presence of the Holy Spirit enables us to deal with Satan and his evil spirits. Satan will do all he can to draw us away from the Lord. Luke 11:24-26 gives a short discourse on how strong evil spirits can be, even to a person who is trying to faithfully serve Christ. There is a constant battle over our souls. Christ wants to live with us eternally, and Satan wants us to die a second death after the great Judgement Day.

A woman in the crowd cried out to Him and said Jesus' mother's womb that birthed Him and the breasts that fed Him were truly blessed. Jesus replied that those who hear the Word of God and keep it are blessed even greater.

Proof Needed (Luke 11:29-32)

It was difficult for many in Jesus' day to comprehend His divinity and the fact that He was the Son of God. They could not understand when He said the Father sent Him from heaven to earth as they knew Joseph and Mary were His earthly parents. Because of this doubt and confusion, many wanted a sign from heaven that would confirm Jesus' heavenly origin.

Jesus told a large crowd that a sign would not be forthcoming except the sign of Jonah the prophet. Jonah was sent by God to minister to the wicked Ninevites, just as Christ had come for the present generation. Jonah's message was repent or be destroyed, and Jesus' message tells us to repent, confess Christ as the Son of God, and be immersed into Him. Jesus wants us to show remorse for sin and acknowledge Him as our Savior. Jonah's and Jesus' messages both pointed to God's forgiveness and future judgment.

Luke refers to Jonah and Solomon. Jonah had a strong message of repentance for salvation and Solomon was the wisest man to live up to that point. Jesus was more important than Jonah or Solomon as His forgiveness and wisdom is on a much higher plane. Jesus' salvation plan is universal for all who will believe in Him. Our acceptance of Jesus' invitation to come has an eternal value.

If anyone today wants proof that Jesus is God's Son, all they need to do is look at His miraculous conception in a young virgin, His death, burial, resurrection, and ascension back to heaven. God's hand was in everything that happened to Jesus. No further sign should ever be needed to be thoroughly convinced of His divinity.

Light and Darkness (Luke 11:33-36)

When we consider what it would be like to live or work in darkness, we may think of a blind person or a miner working inside a mountain. There is no natural light available. The miner relies on his head light strapped to his helmet to provide light so he can see to perform his task. The blind person may be completely blind where natural or manmade light offers no help.

When we live in sin for Satan, we live in spiritual darkness, as we are blind to God's salvation plan. Jesus said in John 8:12, "I am the Light of the world: he that followeth me shall not walk in darkness but shall have the light of life." Once we find His light that changes our life completely, we are obligated to let our light shine to others who do not believe. We are told to not hide our light but let it shine openly for all to see the light of God's truth, mercy, and grace. Light is received through our eyes to drive out darkness. We have been commissioned to let our light shine so other's eyes may be opened to the wonders of serving Christ.

It doesn't take a seminary degree to let our light shine. The most humble person with a limited education can be a strong witness for the Lord. We can tell others what Christ means to us and what He has done for us without even quoting one scripture verse. It is best, of course, to be able to reinforce what we are saying with scripture, but it is not always necessary. Your life and example may be the only Bible some may have as their guide to God.

The Educated and the Elevated (Luke 11:37-54)

Luke talks about the lawyers and Pharisees to give a warning. Lawyers were highly educated and Pharisees were the leading citizens of Israel. They dressed better than the average person, and this showed their superior position. Being a lawyer or a Pharisee did not mean these men should be condemned for their privileged position, as many of them were God-fearing people.

A Pharisee asked Jesus to have a meal with him, so Jesus accepted his invitation. Jesus did not follow the Jewish custom of washing before He ate, and the Pharisee was surprised at this and must have commented to Him about breaking their custom. Jesus told the Pharisee they make the outside clean while their inside is full of greed and wickedness. He said they gave alms to the poor and then considered themselves to be clean. Jesus said they paid tithes of their harvest while overlooking God's justice and love. He told the Pharisee they should definitely continue doing the things they were doing right, but they also needed to look to God for His blessings on their efforts.

Jesus gave the Pharisee a further warning that they prefer the best seats in the synagogue and pleasant greetings in the marketplace. He said the scribes and Pharisees were like unseen graves where men walk over them and do not even realize they are on a grave.

A lawyer also heard Jesus' warning and objected to what He said. He told Jesus it was a reproach to hear Him pronounce judgment. This gave Jesus the opportunity to also rebuke the lawyer when He told him they over-burdened men with a load too heavy to carry. The lawyers did not do anything to help with the burden or to lessen the load. They built tombs for the prophets who were killed by the lawyer's fathers. The lawyers approved of their fathers killing the prophets when they built tombs to hold their dead bodies. Jesus told the lawyers the blood of all the slain prophets for all generations was on their hands. The present generation would pay for all the slain prophets.

The Pharisees and scribes got very upset and cross-examined Jesus on many things as if He had committed a crime. They laid in wait for Jesus to say something so they could accuse Him.

Chapter Nine
The Need for Confession

In Luke 12, there was a large crowd that could not be numbered who came to see and hear Jesus. It was almost like a riot as some were trampled. Jesus told them forthright in Luke 12:1, "Beware of the leaven of the Pharisee, which is hypocrisy." Their attitude was like bread that is fermenting and rising because they were so agitated to the point of violence. Yeast and hypocrisy are alike in that a little affects a lot of dough or people who need Christ. He told the many disciples that nothing (*evil hypocrisy*) is covered up that will not be revealed. Neither they nor we can hide our sins from God as they will be exposed one day in God's final judgment.

It is normal to try and hide our sins from God. When Adam and Eve committed man's first sin, they covered their nakedness and tried to hide from God (Genesis 3:8). Proverbs 28:13 says, "He that covereth his sins shall not prosper: but whoso confesseth and forsaketh them shall prosper." What we consider as "secret sins" may be hidden from men, but not from God. Sins committed in total darkness are as if they were committed in broad daylight in God's eyes. The best recourse we have is to confess our sins so He will forgive as promised; for He is faithful to forgive. (1 John 1:9) Jesus told them even what they whispered would be shouted from the housetops.

Fear and Confession (Luke 12:4-7)

There are two major types of fear: fear of man and circumstances, and the fear of God. Fear is a normal reaction when we face an unknown situation. It may be a human enemy or a major problem that creates fear due to an unknown outcome. The fear of God is different from our human fears, for we feel so insufficient in God's presence. We fear the God who has ultimate power over death and hell. We know our unworthiness due to sin and failure. Perhaps we have knowingly followed Christ at a distance rather than walking closely by His side each day. We may fear Him because of a weakened relationship.

Fear can paralyze us and make it difficult to take positive actions. We must find extra strength to face fear head-on so we can be an overcomer. There will be times when it is impossible to find this strength on our own, so we turn to the one who has the power to overcome sin and death. Jesus wants us to turn to Him so He can turn fear into victory.

Jesus told the large crowd in Luke 12:4, "Be not afraid of them that kill the body and after that have no more that they can do. But I forewarn you whom ye shall fear: Fear him, which after he hath killed hath power to cast into hell; yea, I say unto you, Fear him." We are to fear Satan who can rob us of eternal life with Christ. Solomon tells us in Proverbs 29:25, "The fear of man brings a snare, but whoever trusts in the LORD shall be safe." Our trust in God can help us avoid the trap Satan sets to lure us back into sin.

Jesus told the crowd that five sparrows can be sold for only two copper coins, but God does not forget any of them. He said the hairs on our head are numbered. We don't need to fear for we are of more value in God's eyes than the unforgotten sparrows that fall. Man is preeminent or superior to the fowls, so every person is precious in God's eyes, as He knows each person on first-name basis.

Confessing Christ Publicly (Luke 12:8-12)

Every person is called upon to openly confess Jesus as the Son of God. This is a part of our accepting Him as our Savior. We are sinners and repent of our sins; then we confess Christ before men as we acknowledge Him as the divine Son of God. We make a major change as we turn from sin to follow Christ. This is a lifetime commitment to serve Him faithfully for the rest of our days on earth. Jesus promises when we confess Him before men, He will confess knowing us before the angels of God. We are then baptized into Christ through immersion to replicate His death, burial, and resurrection. If we reject, disown, and deny Christ, we will be disowned, denied, rejected, and refused by Christ before the angels. We have the option to accept or reject Christ.

Jesus states further that if we speak a word against Him, we can be forgiven; but the one who blasphemes against the Holy Spirit will not be forgiven. We cannot deny the work of the Holy Spirit while we claim to be following Christ. When we disown the Holy Spirit, we come up short; and for that there is no forgiveness.

Christ told His disciples to not be afraid when they would be brought before the authorities. He told them to not be anxious and try to craft an answer of defense beforehand. The Holy Spirit would teach them how to reply at the moment they were being interrogated. These disciples had been forewarned by Jesus previously they would face trying times as they went out as missionaries. Their message and faith would be challenged, as they would face persecution and even death.

The prophets, leaders, and apostles were told to "Fear not" on numerous occasions throughout the Scriptures. This reassurance is still in force for every Christian today. With God we can face tomorrow with less fear, stress, and anxiety as we know He loves and cares for each of His children.

Jesus told His disciples in Luke 12:22-34 to not worry about their life or what they would eat or wear. He said life is more than food and clothing. It has been said that the beginning of worry is the end of faith, and the beginning of faith is the end of worry. Every person has concerns, so it is difficult to dismiss worry totally; but we are encouraged to lean on our faith in times of stress.

Jesus used birds as an object lesson. He said the ravens don't sow or reap, they don't have a barn or silo for food storage, and yet God feeds them daily. Then He stated emphatically that man is much more important in God's eyes than the birds! Sometimes we need to learn to turn our problems and cares over to God, for He is in complete control.

We cannot add one inch to our height or one hour to our life. He asks, "Why are you anxious and troubled with cares about the rest?" He then compares our life on earth to the lilies in the field. They don't toil, spin, or weave, but Jesus said they are more magnificent than Solomon in his royal garb. God provides grass that is beautiful today and tomorrow it is thrown into the fire as it has withered and died. Our life on earth is temporary as it flourishes for a while, and then it is gone. Jesus asked how much more God will clothe us who have a weak faith.

Jesus teaches us to not seek material needs such as food and clothing. We are not to worry about these necessities because our Father already knows our needs. He clearly tells us in Luke 12:31, "But rather seek ye first the kingdom of God; and all these things shall be added unto you." Jesus called His followers a little flock when He said to not fear, for it is His Father's intent and good pleasure to give us the kingdom.

He told them to generously share with those in need as our treasure is in heaven. Our personal treasure in heaven cannot evaporate, get damaged, or be stolen by a thief. Our spiritual treasures are securely guarded by God and they are reserved for us in heaven. Jesus concluded by saying in Luke 12:34, "For where your treasure is, there will be your heart also."

The Rich Fool (Luke 12:13-21)

A person in the crowd asked Jesus to tell his brother to share his inheritance with him. Jesus let the man know God had not appointed Him to be a judge of earthly disagreements or an arbiter/umpire of disputes. The man needed to take his case to the courts of law for a decision. Jesus told him that his life consisted of more than the abundance of his possessions.

He then told a parable about a rich and very successful farmer who felt self-sufficient. He was lax and irreverent toward God. The farmer's crop was more bountiful than normal and he did not have enough storage space to hold the harvest. He took a very selfish approach to solve his problem. He decided to tear down his small barns and build larger ones. He would safely store all his crops and then take life easy for many years. He would enjoy life to the fullest as he would eat the best foods and drink choice wines. He wouldn't have a care in the world.

But God said in Luke 12:20, "Thou fool, this night thy soul shall be required of thee: then whose shall those things be, which thou hast provided?" This short lesson points out the foolishness of placing too much value on our possessions. Life is brief, fragile, and uncertain, so it behooves us to have our heart right with God.

Servants (Luke 12:35-48)

Servanthood is a part of our walk with Christ. We come to Him so we can serve Him and our fellow man. When Jesus spoke about the faithful and unfaithful servants in Luke 12:35-40, He was referring to the time He will come back to rapture His church in the end time. He is telling all His children (*servants*) to be ready for His return. We don't know if He will come in the day or at night, so we must be ready for the Master's coming at any time. Those who are watching for His coming will be blessed because of their faithfulness to the end. Those who are not prepared and are not watching will be punished and left behind.

When Jesus comes and finds the faithful watching, He will come as our servant to feed us on His blessings. At that point, we will be His guests and Christ will be the Servant. If we aren't ready for His coming, it will be like a thief that breaks into our house unexpectedly. If we had known the thief was coming, we would have been watching for him so we could protect our house. Jesus wants every person to be alert and watching for His return because it is God's desire that no one perishes in sin.

Luke 12:44 says that if Jesus finds us watching for His coming, He will make us a ruler over what He has. The unfaithful and unprepared will not be allowed into heaven but will be sent away to be with all other unbelievers. We have the message from Luke and other writers that Jesus is coming back. When we have this knowledge, we are expected to be ready for His return. Luke 12:48 tells us if we have been given much, then much shall be required: and to whom men have committed much, of him they will ask the more. We have the knowledge and know Jesus is coming again!

<u>Division and Peace</u> (Luke 12:49-53 and Luke 12:57-59)

Jesus' mission in coming from heaven to earth was to seek and to save sinners. (Luke 9:56) He did not come to destroy, but to save. Every person has the choice of accepting or rejecting Christ after hearing the Gospel. It is Jesus' desire that all men everywhere turn to Him and be saved from their sins.

Jesus looks forward to the day when all God's children will gather around His throne in heaven and praise Him for His goodness, mercy, and salvation; but a separation and cleansing of the earth must take place first. Peter tells us in 2 Peter 3:10 that Jesus will come back as a thief and the heavens (*planets, stars, etc.*) will melt with intense heat. The earth and all signs of sin will also burn up.

Jesus came to bring division between the believers and unbelievers (Luke 12:51). He said He will send fire on the earth. He did not come to bring peace on earth (*in our lifetime*), but division. Families will be divided as children and parents will no longer be united as one. This is a part of God's end time plan. Now is the time to make peace with our enemies and adversaries while we have the opportunity. It will be too late to make peace with Jesus or our enemies after He returns.

Jesus said in Luke 12:54-56 that the hypocrites do not realize the time of His return is imminent. A disbeliever may not realize how quickly Jesus can return without any forewarning. Now is the time to prepare for His coming.

Chapter Ten
Jesus' Parables and Predictions

Jesus often taught by using something people could easily relate to, and He would apply a spiritual heavenly meaning to His lesson. These familiar themes are referred to as parables that were an earthly story with a heavenly meaning. Jesus taught three important parables in Luke 13.

No one can claim they have never sinned. Jesus came to save sinners so we can enjoy eternity with Him. We must come in repentance so Christ will forgive our sins. Jesus lays it out clearly when He said we must repent or perish. Repentance gives us immunity from God's judgment.

Parable of the Fig Tree (Luke 13:6-9)

This parable is about a man who had a fig tree that refused to bear fruit. He patiently waited on the tree to yield fruit, but he was deeply disappointed. The orchard owner told the care taker to cut down the tree as it had been barren for three consecutive years. The care taker convinced the owner to let him work with the tree to see if he could encourage it to bear fruit. He would go the extra mile by digging around and feeding it. The caretaker did not want to lose the tree.

The parable refers to God, our spiritual orchard owner. We see Christ as the care taker over our spiritual well-being. He is patient and long-suffering as it is His desire that we bear much fruit for God. He is our Intercessor and Mediator with God as He pleads our case for a second chance.

One day God will deal with the spiritually dead, the unproductive, and all sinners by casting them in the lake of fire with Satan. God has no place for the person who ignores and fails to follow Him. God expects us to bear fruits of repentance so others will see what Christ means to us. (Psalm 11:6)

Healing on the Sabbath (Luke 13:10-17)

Jesus was always on call to help the lame, diseased, blind, those possessed with evil spirits, etc. He healed the sick when He came in contact with them regardless of what day of the week it was. The Pharisees observed the Sabbath Law religiously and claimed they did no work on that day of the week, but Jesus knew better. Jesus encountered a woman with a defective spine in the synagogue on the Sabbath. She had been unable to stand straight for eighteen years. Jesus had compassion on her and said in Luke 13:12, "Woman, thou art loosed from thine infirmity." He laid His hands on the woman and she immediately stood tall and glorified God.

The ruler in the synagogue was indignant because Jesus healed on the Sabbath. There was no compassion for the woman who needed Jesus' healing touch. The ruler told Jesus He had six days a week to heal, but He should not heal on the Sabbath. Jesus called the ruler a hypocrite because the Jews would free their animals on the Sabbath so they could go drink. He told the ruler the woman had been bound by Satan for eighteen years and asked if she should not be loosed from her bondage on the Sabbath. The ruler was ashamed, but the people rejoiced for the miraculous things Jesus did.

This should serve as a warning to every believer. It is easy to get distracted by man's rules and forget how Christ wants us to show compassion every day. We need to always keep the main thing the main thing.

Mustard Seed and Leaven (Luke 13:18-21)

The parables of the mustard seed and leaven will be addressed jointly since they are so similar. The mustard seed is tiny, and it only takes a very small amount of yeast to make the entire lump of dough rise. Size or amount does not matter to God as we can impact other's lives when we are willing to invest in them.

Jesus taught that the kingdom of God is like the mustard seed. When it was planted, it grew into such a large tree that the birds could nest in it. We are small and weak instruments when compared to God, but He can take what we have and multiply it into a blessing to others. We may think our talent is too small or non-existent to be of any use to God, but it is amazing what He can do when we place ourself in His service and ask Him to use us to bless others. We should never under-estimate God's unlimited power.

Yeast consists of tiny cells of various fungi that bakers use to make delicious bread and pastries. Galatians 5:9 says, "A little leaven leavens the whole lump." Melt-in-your-mouth rolls or cake would not be worth eating without leaven. The yeast changes a blob of dough into something that makes us want more. Our lives are like the yeast. We may feel small or weak, but we can bless others in a large way. In a church, the Holy Spirit is like the leaven. Without His presence and direction, the church cannot be a blessing to others. When the Spirit is present in a church, doors of opportunity for service to others will be opened.

The Narrow Gate (Luke 13:22-33)

This lesson from Jesus is sad, for it depicts those who will be lost to Satan. Jesus used the imagery of a narrow gate that represents those who carry a heavy burden of unforgiven sin who would like to enter into His kingdom. They are unable to pass through the gate because they have refused to lay their heavy load of sin at Jesus' feet so they can be forgiven. Only the forgiven will be able to enter into God's kingdom. Each person can decide their fate when it comes to God's forgiveness. John 3:16 says whosoever will, may come.

One day the Master of the house will close the door to forgiveness. The people on the outside of Noah's ark refused to hear and heed Noah's message, but when God shut the door and sent the great flood, only Noah and his family were saved. Everyone outside the ark had refused to heed his message of salvation.

The Gospel is taught and preached today from the pulpit and the media. There are more opportunities for people to hear the Gospel today than ever. Some are receptive while others ignore the opportunity to come to Christ in repentance to receive Him. He alone has forgiving power that can make sinners into saints. He said in John 14:6, "I am the way, the truth, and the life: no man cometh to the Father, but by me." Jesus is the narrow gate we must pass through if we want to get to God the Father.

When Jesus comes back, the door for forgiveness will be shut. Men may call on God to open the door, but it will be too late. God will say, "Depart from me, ye cursed, into everlasting fire." (Matthew 25:41) We may remind God how we attended church, listened to the messages, and did good deeds, but this won't matter if we do not repent of our sins and confess Christ as the Son of God.

When the Pharisees heard Jesus teach so sternly, they told Him to leave as Herod intended to kill Him. Jesus called Herod a fox and told the Pharisees to tell Herod that He would continue to perform miracles. Then Jesus said on the third day, He would be perfected, referring to His upcoming resurrection on the third day after His crucifixion.

Jesus' Sorrow (Luke 13:34-35)

Jesus loved the city of Jerusalem. It was the city where Jews came from all over the kingdom to celebrate the holy festivals and feast days throughout the year. Jerusalem is where Jesus was found in the temple at the young age of twelve consulting with the religious leaders. Jesus had stood up for what was right in Jerusalem when He took a firm stand against evil on several occasions. It was a special place for Jesus.

He felt a sense of pride and compassion for the citizens who lived in the city. Jesus often wanted to gather them under His wings for protection like a mother hen gathers her chicks under her wings when a storm is approaching, but they would not heed His message (Matthew 23:37). They had killed the prophets and stoned those who brought God's message of love to them, but Jesus still loved them. Their spiritual houses stood in desolation, but Jesus told them the day would come when they would say, "Blessed is He that cometh in the name of the Lord." Our challenge is to be sure our spiritual house is in good order because of a close relationship with the Lord.

Chapter Eleven
Humility and Commitment

When we hear the Gospel and realize our lost condition, we humbly come to Christ in repentance. Our coming to Christ is similar to marriage, for it is a lifetime commitment. Jesus expects us to walk with him every day regardless of feelings or circumstances. We are to submit ourselves as living sacrifices to be used in His kingdom work. Romans 12:1 urges us to present our bodies a living sacrifice, holy, acceptable unto God, which is our reasonable service. Jesus gave His all to die as our sacrificial lamb, but we are a living sacrifice that we offer to God. A full commitment is the reasonable thing to do.

Luke 14:1-6 finds Jesus eating with another ruler of the Pharisees on the Sabbath. His critics watched closely as they loved to ridicule Jesus for eating with Pharisees, lawyers, tax collectors, and sinners. A man with dropsy (*an accumulation of watery fluid*) was in Jesus' presence and he needed to be healed. Jesus asked the lawyers if it was legal for Him to heal on the Sabbath. They did not answer Jesus' question, so He healed the man and sent him away. Jesus then asked the lawyers if they had an animal that fell in a pit on the Sabbath, would they not pull him out. The Pharisees did necessary work on the Sabbath, so they had no grounds to condemn Jesus for healing on the Sabbath.

Humility (Luke 14:7-14)

Jesus taught them a parable about the seating order at a wedding feast. He told them when they entered the banquet hall they should not take the best seats at the table as someone more honorable may come to the feast. If they sat in the best seats and were asked to move, they would be embarrassed when asked to take a less important seat. Jesus said it is better to enter and take the lowest seat hoping the host of the banquet would ask them to move to a more desirable seat. The other guests at the table would then look upon them favorably as the host gave them better seats. Jesus drove home His point on humility in Luke 14:11 when He said, "For whosoever exalteth himself shall be abased; and he that humbleth himself shall be exalted."

Jesus told them further that when they gave a feast to not invite their friends, family members, or neighbors. He told them they should invite the poor, maimed, lame, and blind to their feast. They were promised blessings by Jesus for they would give without expecting a return. He told them they would be repaid on the saint's resurrection day.

Another parable about humility is recorded in Luke 14:15-24. A man put on a lavish supper and invited many of his friends. When it was time to eat and everything was ready, the man sent his servant to invite his friends to come to supper. All his friends insulted the host by making excuses on why they could not come. One man said he had bought a piece of ground and needed to go see it. Another said he had bought five yoke of oxen and needed to go test them. The third man said he had just gotten married and could not come.

When the servant told his master none of his friends were coming to supper, the host got very upset. He angrily told his servant to go out and bring in the poor, maimed, lame, and blind to the lavish supper. The servant obeyed and brought as many as he could find, but there were still empty seats at the table. The master told his servant to go out and compel others to come so the table would be filled. The ones who made excuses and refused to come would suffer the loss.

The application of this parable is very important. The master of the feast is Jesus Christ and His call to come to supper is universal. Now is the accepted time to come to the spiritual feast without delay. Jesus calls all men to repent and come to enjoy the spiritual blessings He has promised. We cannot make excuses for refusing to come if we want His blessings of forgiveness, spiritual healing, and the hope of eternal life with Him. The poor, maimed, lame, and blind represent the outcasts of society. Jesus loves and invites every person to come regardless of our level of success or failure. He will receive every person who humbly comes without exception. Jesus expects every one of His children to be like the servant who issued the invitation to come. What an opportunity to be a personal representative of Christ when we invite others to come to His spiritual feast of blessings.

Sacrifice (Luke 14:25-33)

When we accept Christ as our Savior, we are like the military recruit who leaves family and friends to serve his/her country. We forsake all and accept full responsibility to sacrifice whatever it takes to serve our loving Lord without hesitation or reluctance. Christ sacrificed His life on the cross so we can find salvation in Him. We in turn make sacrifices so we can make a full commitment and serve in His royal army. Soldiers are workers, not shirkers; and so it is in our service for Christ.

Jesus told the crowd of followers that if they did not make a full sacrifice they could not be one of His. He said we must forsake our family members and even sacrifice our life to be His disciple. Jesus demands our full allegiance if we are to be one of His soldiers. He said if we cannot bear our cross and come to Him, we cannot be His disciple. He instructs us to count the cost of discipleship before we embark on our journey with Him. It doesn't do anyone any good to begin our journey with Christ full of excitement if our commitment is not real and genuine. We bring criticism and shame upon ourselves to have a strong start that soon fizzles when trials come.

He tells us we must be like a king who commits soldiers to battle before knowing how strong the enemy army may be. The king cannot afford to back down when he learns his troops are outnumbered. People will call him a weakling leader who backs out when challenged. Jesus made a strong point when He said in Luke 14:33, "Whosoever he that forsaketh not all that he hath, he cannot be my disciple." We must forsake all sin and associations that will be a detriment in our service to Christ.

Jesus closes this lesson by saying we are like salt that is used to preserve and flavor food. When salt loses its flavor, it is not good for anything. The same is true for the person who starts strong for Christ and then withdraws when times get tough. We cannot add anything to Christ and His kingdom unless we stay actively engaged in His service.

Chapter Twelve
Losing and Gaining

Luke records three powerful parables of Jesus in Luke 15, and all three parables are about loss. Every person has probably experienced the loss of something of value. There is anxiety mixed with hope as we search to find what we lost.

The Lost Sheep (Luke 15:4-7)

Jesus' audience included the Pharisees, scribes, tax collectors, and sinners. This was a teaching opportunity to reach those who opposed Him. They accused Jesus of eating with sinners, so He taught them about a lost sheep.

He asked them if they had a hundred sheep and lost one of them, would they not leave the ninety-nine and go find the one lost sheep. They would search until they found the lost sheep, place it on their shoulders, and bring it back to the flock. There would be great rejoicing by his friends and neighbors when they learned about how the shepherd did the right thing in finding his lost sheep. Jesus' point was that there is more rejoicing in heaven over one sinner who repents than over ninety-nine persons who need no repentance.

Christ is our true and good Shepherd and we are His sheep. When one person is outside the flock of God, Jesus seeks to find the lost one to bring them into the fold. The lost sheep may be a person who has never accepted Christ, or a believer who strayed from their commitment to Him. It is easy to let the cares of this world distract us from keeping our commitment to Christ. Jesus stands ready to grant second chances to the person who started strong but strayed.

The Lost Coin (Luke 15:8-10)

The first two parables Jesus taught in Luke 15 are very brief but are strong lessons that deserve our full attention. A woman had ten coins but lost one of them. She lit a lamp and swept her house until she found the lost coin. When she found the coin, she called her friends and neighbors together to rejoice with them over the coin she found. Jesus closed the parable by saying there is great joy among the angels in heaven over one sinner who repents.

The lost coin did not lose its value while it was lost, just as a sinner's soul while they are outside of Christ. Every saint or sinner is worthy of salvation through Christ. We are all valuable in the eyes of the Lord and deserve to be found and restored into a right relationship with Him. The vilest sinner can find forgiveness, peace, and restoration when they come to Christ.

The Lost Son (Luke 15:11-32)

The parable of the prodigal son is one of Jesus' most familiar discourses. It goes from a unified family to a broken family to a re-united family. The emotions run from disappointment and broken hearts to pure joy and elation. In this parable, we see Jesus as the father and sinners as the prodigal. A prodigal is one who lives their daily life with loose and immoral living. Every person has played the role of the prodigal when we were unsaved or drifted away from Christ. The parable shows us the need for repentance and a return to Christ.

A farmer had two sons who worked with him. The older son apparently was satisfied with his situation as he faithfully worked diligently for his father each day. The younger son wanted no part of working on the farm, so he decided on a major lifestyle change. He demanded his inheritance although his father was still living. This was an insult to the father that his son would demand his inheritance while he was still alive. He was going to take his money and leave home. The father must have been heartbroken that his son would make such a demand; but he did what was necessary to give the son his unearned inheritance. He may have needed to sell land or other assets to come up with the cash. The son gathered his belongings and left home. The father must have been very sad as he watched his son leave.

The young man went to a distant country and found new friends. He lived it up as he partied with wine, women, and song. It didn't take long for the money to run out, and his "friends" disappeared. He had been extravagantly wasteful, and now he was flat broke. A famine hit the land and the young man didn't have two coins to rub together. He didn't have any money left to even buy a piece of bread.

A pig farmer gave him the job of feeding vegetable pods to his swine. A pod is like a green bean, a pea, or some other dried vegetable with a bean inside. His hunger pangs were so severe he could have eaten the pods, but no one gave him anything to eat. His life of excess quickly turned into a desolate situation. When he hit rock bottom, he came to his senses and realized his father's hired farm hands had spare food and here he was starving to death in a stinking pig sty.

He felt a need to repent to his dad, so he decided to return home and ask his father to forgive him and let him work as a hired servant as He was unworthy to be restored as a son. He started toward home to seek his father's forgiveness. The father looked a great distance down the road and saw his pitiful son coming home. He probably reeked of the odor from the pig sty and he, no doubt, needed a hot bath. His sandals were worn out and his eyes had sunk into his skull from not eating. His dad had compassion when he saw his son, so he ran to meet him, hugged, and kissed him. The son said, "Father, I have sinned against heaven and against you. I am no longer worthy to be called your son."

The father had his servants bring the best robe, a ring for his finger, and new sandals. The robe represented royalty and the ring showed the father's unending love. They killed a calf and had a feast to celebrate the son's return. The dad said, "This son of mine was dead and is alive again; he was lost and is found!" The young man was restored as a son, as his sins had been forgiven.

This parable is the picture of a wayward sinner who has turned his back on Christ. Selfish ambitions overrode a relationship with Christ, while physical appetites and lusts were filled. Christ gives us the option to go or stay. Sooner or later life has a way of showing us the error of our ways. Christ is always ready with forgiveness when we return.

There is more to the story. The older son got angry that his young brother's return was being celebrated with feasting, music, and dancing. He refused to go to the party and celebrate his brother's return. He told his father he had slaved for him for several years and he had never even received a goat so he could celebrate with his friends. The younger son had squandered his father's estate with prostitutes, and yet the father celebrated. The dad reminded his oldest son that his brother was dead but was alive again; he was lost and had been found.

Jesus stands today looking down the road for the return of prodigal sons. It doesn't matter to Him what sins we have committed, He stands with open arms ready to forgive, cleanse, and restore. There is great joy in heaven when a sinner comes home.

The Unjust Steward (Luke 16:1-13)

Jesus continues with another parable. A wealthy man had a manager who oversaw his estate. A claim was made against the manager that he was squandering his master's assets. The owner called the wasteful manager in and asked him what had been going on, and he fired him on the spot. The manager quickly realized his predicament. He could not labor with his hands as he had been doing office work, and he was too ashamed to beg.

He decided that perhaps his master's debtors would take him into their homes. The manager asked each debtor how much they owed the owner of the estate. One debtor owed 900 gallons (*about 3,000 liters*) of oil and another owed 900 bushels (*about 20 tons*) of wheat. The fired manager told them to reduce the acknowledgment of their debt documents to 450 gallons of oil and 700 bushels of wheat.

The owner did not condone what the manager had done to waste his estate, but he commended him for being shrewd with his debtors. Jesus was teaching that we are not to use worldly gains to satisfy personal desires, but we should use our resources for things of eternal value. God will reward us for our generosity in helping our friends with sacrificial gifts. The way we use what God has entrusted to us defines the sincerity of discipleship.

Jesus closes the parable of the unjust steward by saying we cannot serve two masters. He was referring to God and money. He said we will love one and hate the other or we will be devoted to one and despise the other. The desires of our hearts will be revealed in the light of God's truth. The Pharisees loved money, so they began to sneer, scoff, and ridicule Jesus for His statement about the love of money. Jesus told them they justified and defended their actions before men, but God knew their hearts. What greedy man approves, God detests.

The Law and the prophets existed until the time of John the Baptist, but now the kingdom of God was being preached. John the Baptist was the pivot or transition point from the old to the new. Jesus came to provide continuity from the Law to His period of grace and mercy. He came to fulfill the Law the Pharisees and Jews used as their standard for living. John the Baptist's coming opened the way to God through Jesus His Son. The Law was their master, but Jesus is now our Mediator and Intercessor.

The Pharisees added many amendments to the Ten Commandments. One of their amendments related to divorce. They were quite liberal by allowing trivial reasons for divorce. Jesus gave the Law a more rigid interpretation by saying adultery is the only reason for divorce.

The Rich Man and Lazarus (Luke 16:19-31)

There were two men who were polar opposites. One was wealthy and the other was dirt poor. The rich man lived in luxury; he wore the best clothing and ate only the finest foods each day. He totally disregarded God's impending judgment. Lazarus was a poor beggar who was laid at the rich man's gate daily. His body was covered with sores that the dogs would lick to give him a small degree of comfort. He was constantly hungry and only wanted the crumbs that fell from the rich man's table; but his needs were ignored.

The beggar died and the angels carried him to Abraham's bosom in Paradise where he feasted. The rich man also died and was buried. No doubt, he had an elaborate funeral due to his wealth and many friends. The rich man was in torment in Hades when he saw Lazarus and Abraham a great distance away. The rich man was burning in flames, and he begged Abraham to send Lazarus so he could dip his finger in cool water to place on his burning tongue. Abraham reminded the rich man he received many good things while alive on earth while Lazarus suffered greatly. Abraham told the rich man Lazarus was now being comforted while he was being tormented.

There was a wide gulf between Abraham and Hades where the rich man had instantly become poor when he died. Lazarus had transitioned from abject poverty to the riches of eternity when he died. No one could travel across the wide gulf as each of their eternal destinations was fixed by God.

The man in Hades begged Abraham to send Lazarus to tell his brothers about the awful place of torment where he suffered endlessly. He wanted to spare his brothers of the pain he suffered and the awful place of fire and torment. Abraham told him his brothers had Moses and the prophets who warned them about Hades, but they did not listen. The man persisted and said his brothers may listen and repent if someone from the dead went to them, but Abraham refused his request.

God loves us so much that He sent His only Son from heaven to earth to die and pay our sin debt. His love and forgiveness is extended and is available to all who seek Him. We must decide in this life whether to accept Christ as our Lord as it is too late after death.

Chapter Thirteen
Jesus' Return

Forgiveness (Luke 17:1-4)

Forgiveness is an essential part of being a Christian. When we receive forgiveness of sin from Christ, we are to then practice forgiveness when our fellow man sins against us. Peter asked Jesus in Matthew 18:21-22 how many times he should forgive someone. Should he forgive him seven times? Jesus told Peter he should forgive seventy times seven. Jesus taught Peter the concept of forgiving without limits.

Jesus issued a warning to His disciples in Luke 17 for those who set traps to entice others to sin. He said it would be better for a millstone to be tied around the tempter's neck and be cast into the sea, rather than cause someone to sin. It is easy for the spiritually weak to be lured into sin. We must study the Bible and seek God through prayer to increase our spiritual stamina so we can find strength to resist temptation.

We are taught to help each other live exemplary lives. If someone falls into Satan's trap of temptation and sins, we are to reprove and encourage them to do better. If he commits sin against us multiple times but seeks our forgiveness, we are to forgive and cancel his sin without hesitation each time he repents. Paul tells us in Ephesians 4:32 to be kind to one another, tender-hearted, forgiving, even as God through Christ has forgiven us. We reflect God's forgiveness when we forgive others. Colossians 3:13 sums forgiveness up by saying, "Forbearing one another, and forgiving one another, if any man has a quarrel against any: even as Christ forgave you, so also do ye."

The Need for Faith (Luke 17:5-10)

Our Christian journey is a walk of faith. Faith enables us to believe in someone or something we cannot see. Many of God's children have a need for stronger faith. His plan is laid out for us in the Scriptures, but it takes faith to step out to follow Him to places unknown.

Abraham and Sarah were perfect examples of having blind faith. In Genesis 12:1, God told Abraham when he was seventy-five years old to pack up and leave home but didn't tell him specifically where to go in the land of Canaan.

Abraham had faith that when they arrived at God's appointed destination, he would know it.

Then God challenged Abraham's faith again in Genesis 22:2-13 to take his only son, Isaac, to the land of Moriah and offer him as a sacrifice. Abraham, Isaac, and their travel partners journeyed for three days to the mountain. Abraham bound Isaac and laid him on the altar. He drew the knife back to stab his son when a voice from heaven told him to stop. God provided a ram caught in the thicket as a sacrifice. Abraham proved his faith to God through unquestioning obedience.

The apostles asked Jesus in Luke 17:5 to increase their faith. They were getting ready to scatter and go to parts unknown as missionaries. Jesus said if they had a tiny amount of faith that was compared to a small mustard seed; they would be able to do miraculous things. He referred to His apostles as servants who would serve their Master and fellow man. Service to others takes patience and faith, and sometimes it is a thankless job. No matter how much we are underappreciated, we still serve in faith that something good will happen in the other person's life. It is a high honor to be a servant in

God's kingdom work. God expects us to go beyond our perceived obligation because that is our duty to Him.

Jesus demonstrated what it is like to do good deeds that go unnoticed. He was at the border of Samaria and Galilee where He met ten lepers. The men called out to Jesus for mercy and healing. Jesus looked on these sick men with pity and healed all ten. After the men went to the priest, one realized he had been healed so he went back to thank Jesus for being cured of this dreaded disease. He thanked and praised God with a loud voice. He fell prostrate at Jesus' feet and thanked Him repeatedly. Jesus asked him where the other nine men were that He healed. They accepted healing without one ounce of gratitude. Jesus told the man his faith had restored his health.

Jesus' Return (Luke 17:20-37)

The second coming of Christ to rapture His church is like a golden thread that runs throughout the Bible. The prophets foretold of Jesus' birth, death, resurrection, and judgment day. A part of Jesus' model prayer in Matthew 6:10 said, "Thy kingdom come, Thy will be done on earth as it is in heaven." Men have looked for His return for centuries, and we still eagerly await His return.

The Pharisees asked Jesus in Luke 17:20 when the kingdom of God would come. He told them the kingdom of God was already in each believer. God's kingdom mentioned here is spiritual, not physical. Jesus told His disciples the day would come when they would want to see Him, but they would not be able to see Him. He said the Son of Man would be like the lightning that flashes across the heavens from one end to the other.

Before Jesus could receive His glorified and eternal body, He must first suffer many things. He would be rejected just as Noah was before the great flood. In Lot's day the people in the wicked cities of Sodom and Gomorrah ate, drank, planted, bought, sold, and built. Everything was normal until the day Lot took his wife and daughters out of the city. That same day God rained fire and brimstone (*hot burning sulphur*) down and destroyed the evil cities and every person.

Jesus said that is how it will be on the day we see the Son of Man coming. The person on the housetop need not go into his house to get his belongings; likewise, the person in the field should not turn back. We need to remember Lot's wife who violated God's command to not look back at the burning cities. She disobeyed and looked back at the burning cities and was instantly turned into a pillar of salt. (Genesis 19:26) Jesus said if we try to preserve our present life, we will lose it, but the ones who are willing to lose their earthly life for His sake, will preserve and keep it alive for eternity.

Good will be separated from evil when He returns. There will be two men in one bed at night; one will be taken and the other will be left behind. There will be two women grinding grain together; one will be taken and the other left behind. There will be two men in the field working side-by-side; one will be taken and the other left behind. They asked Jesus, "Where, Lord?" He told them the vultures and eagles will gather where the dead bodies will be.

The kingdom of God dwells in the hearts of believers. When we pray the Lord's Prayer and say, "Thy kingdom come," that is a present-day desire plus a future event to come. Every believer is a part of God's kingdom on earth. We are automatically accepted into His kingdom when we repent of our sins, confess Jesus as the Son of God, and are baptized into Christ.

Chapter Fourteen
All Things Are Possible

God has proven that all things are possible with Him from the beginning of time. He has the power to create and sustain all things and individuals. He showed His power when the Virgin Mary conceived baby Jesus with no human intervention. His power to allow Jesus to perform one miracle after another cannot be argued. His power to send Jesus back to earth to rapture His church is yet to be seen, but through faith we know He can and will keep His promise. There is no comparison between the unlimited power of God and the limited power of man.

Our Judge (Luke 18:1-8)

Jesus laid the foundation of this brief lesson by saying men should always pray and not lose heart. It is easy to lose heart when we tackle life's problems on our own strength. When we turn to God He can help us navigate our problems and reach an acceptable solution. The answer may not be what we initially desired or prayed for, but God sees the big picture when we only see to the curve ahead.

In this parable, a widow was having trouble with her enemy. Jesus did not say what the problem was, but it doesn't matter as He is powerful enough to deal with the most severe problems. The widow asked the judge to come to her defense, but he was a man who did not fear or reverence God; furthermore, he had no respect for any man. The widow asked the judge to protect and give her justice with her enemy. After repeated appearances before the judge, he finally relented because of her persistence. She was an annoyance to the judge because she would not back off. The judge feared the widow may even attack him with an assault or strangle him if he did not act on her behalf.

Jesus told His followers to pay close attention to what the unjust judge had said. He then asked if our just God will defend, protect, and avenge His elect, or chosen ones, who persistently cry out to Him day and night. Jesus stated that God will defend, protect, and avenge His children speedily. Then Jesus asked if He would find a persistent faith when He comes back to earth.

The Pharisee and the Tax Collector (Luke 18:9-14)

Pharisees were from a Jewish sect during Jesus' time on earth. They were the elite men who dressed to the nines in their fancy robes. The Pharisees took great pride in their leadership role as they felt better than the average citizen. They trusted in themselves, were self-righteous, and looked down on their fellow citizens. Tax collectors worked for the Roman government that ruled over Israel and were disrespected by many.

A Pharisee and a tax collector went into the temple to pray. In Luke 18:11-12, the Pharisee prayed: "God, I thank Thee that I am not as other men are, extortioners (*robbers*), unjust (*swindlers*), adulterers, or even as this publican (*tax collector*). I fast twice in the week, I give tithes of all that I possess." The man had an ego problem when he told God what a good man he was. Instead of coming humbly to pray, he came boastfully to God. He did at least recognize God but he thanked him for his own goodness.

The tax collector, who stood a short distance from the Pharisee, would not even lift up his eyes to heaven. He struck his breast repeatedly and said in Luke 18:13, "God, be merciful to me a sinner." He recognized God as Supreme and himself as a sinner. Humility was more important than ego to the tax collector and certainly to God.

The result was the tax collector went home forgiven and in right standing with God, rather than the Pharisee. Jesus made a strong statement in Luke 18:14 when He said, "Everyone that exalteth himself shall be abased; and he that humbleth himself shall be exalted." Jesus is our example of humility. We have nothing to bring to God except a humble spirit.

Love for Children (Luke 18:15-17)

Jesus loves babies and children. Some parents brought their babies to Jesus one day so He could touch them. His disciples reproved the parents, but Jesus told them it was alright. He said they should allow the little children to come to Him without hindrance, for they are a part of and belong to God's kingdom. He taught that whoever does not welcome the kingdom of God like a little child will have no part in it.

Babies are one of God's greatest gifts to parents. We never know the potential in a little baby. They can mature and contribute much to an imperfect world. Some become world leaders, professionals, military leaders, or religious leaders. Great poets or artists started as little babies. Jesus loves every one of them. They are so pure and innocent.

The Rich Young Ruler (Luke 18:18-23)

A wealthy young ruler approached Jesus with a question. He was perhaps a ruler in the synagogue or a Jewish elder. He called Jesus, "Good teacher" and asked what he must do to inherit eternal life. Jesus told him no one is good except God, and then He asked the ruler if he knew the commandments: don't commit adultery, murder, theft, or give false testimony against others. He also told the ruler he must honor his parents. The ruler said he had done all these commandments since he was a child. Jesus told the ruler he lacked one thing. He should sell all he owned and give to the poor so he would have treasure in heaven. Jesus told him to then come and follow Him.

The very wealthy young ruler was saddened over the instructions Jesus gave. Perhaps he had gained his wealth through an inheritance or shrewd business deals, but Jesus told him to sell it all. Jesus told the ruler it is hard for a rich person to enter the kingdom of God. It is very difficult, but not impossible, for most rich people to sacrifice for Christ or abandon all to follow Him.

The witnesses heard Jesus' response to the young ruler and asked who then can be saved. Jesus told them what is impossible for man is possible with God. Peter reminded Jesus his apostles had left all they had to follow him. Jesus reassured Peter in Luke 18:29-30, "No man that hath left house, parents, brethren, wife, or children for the kingdom of God's sake, who shall not receive manifold more in this present time, and in the world to come life everlasting." Jesus asks us to put things in perspective when it comes to serving Him. Our possessions should not be impediments to our full commitment and service to the Lord.

Jesus then called His disciples aside in Luke 18:31-34 to explain to them again what He was facing. They were going to Jerusalem where the prophet's writings about His last days on earth would be fulfilled. He would be delivered to the Gentiles, be mocked, spitefully treated (*be made sport of*), insulted, spit on, scourged (*flogged*), and killed. On the third day Jesus said He would rise from the dead as prophesied in Psalm 16:10. The disciples did not understand anything Jesus said. How could anyone mistreat Jesus like this after all He had done for so many? He had performed many miracles of healing, casting out demons, giving sight, and had even raised the dead.

The Blind Beggar (Luke 18:35-43)

Jesus started His trek to Jerusalem. As He approached Jericho, He saw a blind beggar by the side of the road. The blind man heard the commotion in the crowd that followed Jesus and asked what was happening. They told him Jesus was passing by. He cried out and begged Jesus to have mercy on him. The leaders in the procession told the blind man to be quiet, but he shouted louder for Jesus to have mercy on him. Jesus stopped and asked the blind man what he wanted Him to do. The man told Jesus he just wanted to see. Jesus told him in Luke 18:42, "Receive thy sight; thy faith hath saved thee."

The man received his sight immediately and gave God the glory. All the people saw what happened and they praised God.

The wealthy young ruler refused to follow Christ, but this blind man, who could now see, had a burning desire to follow Him.

Chapter Fifteen
Triumphant Entry

Luke 19 records Jesus' triumphant entry into the city of Jerusalem. The time for His betrayal, arrest, and crucifixion was drawing near. Jesus knew He was facing a very difficult and crucial moment in His ministry and life on earth.

Visit With a Publican (Luke 19: 1-10)

On His way to Jerusalem, Jesus passed through Jericho. Zacchaeus was a rich tax collector (*publican*) in Jericho. A publican collected taxes, tolls, and other levies for the Roman government. Tax collectors would mark-up the government tax assessments and keep the profit for themselves. This was a lucrative and rewarding job as the publicans built up their personal wealth. They were hated by many who felt the tax collectors gouged them without mercy.

Zacchaeus was not very tall, but he wanted to see Jesus as He made His way through Jericho. He ran ahead of Jesus and climbed up in a tree so he could see Him. Jesus stopped at Zacchaeus' tree and told him to come down, as He was going to his home to eat with Him that day. Zacchaeus climbed down as he was elated that Jesus was going to visit in his home.

The critics saw what was happening and they accused Jesus of eating with a sinner. Jesus had just found a man the citizens judged as a sinner and He would spend time by sharing a meal with him.

Zacchaeus told Jesus he gave half of what he had to the poor, and if he had taken anything illegally from anyone he would pay them back four-fold. Jesus told Zacchaeus salvation had come to his house that day, because Zacchaeus was a son of Abraham. Then Jesus reiterated He came to seek and to save the lost. Jesus gave Zacchaeus hope that day. Although others saw him as a sinner, Jesus saw him as a son.

Parable of Minas (Luke 19:11-27)

Jesus continued to teach by using parables. He was now nearing Jerusalem, and the people thought the kingdom of God would appear immediately. They hoped Jesus would establish a new political or military kingdom, not a spiritual one.

This parable is about a nobleman who went into a distant country to obtain a kingdom for himself and then return home. Before leaving, the nobleman called his bond servants and gave each of them a mina (one hundred days' wages). The nobleman told his servants to buy and sell while he was away.

When he returned home he asked the bond servants to give an account on how they had grown the minas he had given them. He wanted to know the bottom-line profit they had made.

- The first servant used his mina to make a profit of another ten. This pleased the nobleman and he gave the servant authority over ten cities.
- The second servant made a profit of five minas, so the nobleman gave him authority over five cities.
- The third servant told the nobleman he had kept his mina in a handkerchief. He told the nobleman he feared him because he was such a hard, greedy, and stern man. The servant was reprimanded and was told he would judge and condemn him, and he called him a wicked slave. He asked the servant why he did not put the money in

the bank so it would earn interest. They took the mina away from the unproductive servant and gave it to the one with ten minas. The people questioned the nobleman and told him the faithful servant already had ten minas. Jesus said the one who gets and has will be given more, but the person who does not get and does not have, his mina will be taken away.

Jesus closed the parable by saying the nobleman's enemies in the distant country who did not want Him to reign over them should be brought and slaughtered in his presence.

Each child of God has talents we have been given to use in His kingdom work. We have the choice to use our talents so we can receive more talents or sit on and protect them. The message is clear from Jesus: we are to use and grow our talents, or they will be taken away.

<u>Jesus' Entry into Jerusalem</u> (Luke 19:28-40)

Jesus had come to Jerusalem ever since He was a child. He would normally enter the city without fanfare, but this time it was very different. Both excitement and hatred had been swelling for three years, and the culmination of His ministry was nearing.

Jesus left Jericho and proceeded to Jerusalem, God's holy city on earth. When He neared the Mount of Olives, He sent two of His disciples into the village where they would find a colt tied. No human had ever ridden this colt that was to be brought to Jesus. If anyone questioned their actions, they were to tell them the Lord had need of the colt. They found the colt and started untying it when the owners asked what they were doing, and they told the owners what the Lord had said.

The colt was brought to Jesus, and the disciples put some of their clothes on its back. Jesus mounted the colt's back and started down the mountain toward the city of Jerusalem. Zechariah 9:9 tells us the prophecy that Jesus quoted in Matthew 21:5, "Behold, thy King cometh unto thee, meek, and sitting upon an ass, and a colt, the foal of an ass." Matthew 21:8 says the people in the crowd around Jesus laid their clothes and palm branches in the path of the colt. They treated Him like a king coming in victory to establish His kingdom.

As he neared the descent from the Mount of Olives to Jerusalem, the entire crowd began to rejoice and praise God loudly for the powerful works and miracles they had seen. They shouted in unison, "Blessed is the King who comes in the name of the LORD! Peace in heaven and glory in the highest!" They heaped praise on the God of heaven where freedom reigns. There would be no more distress over the things of this world. Some of the Pharisees in the crowd asked Jesus to reprove His disciples, as things were getting out of hand. Jesus told them if He asked them to be silent, the stones would cry out (*praising God*).

Jesus looked down upon Jerusalem and wept audibly over it because of her spiritual blindness to the blessings they could have found in Him. They had missed the peace and security they could have enjoyed if they had only believed in Him. As a result, their enemy would surround the city in the future, and build high banks to cut Jerusalem off from the outside world. Jesus told them the enemy would destroy the city and not leave one stone on top of another simply because of their rejection of Him.

Jesus arrived at the temple and went inside. He saw the vendors selling sacrificial animals and the temple currency changers conducting business in the temple as if they were in a place of commerce. He did not object to their providing a service to the worshipers coming from distant parts, but they should not be doing business in the temple. He told them the temple was a place of prayer, but they had made it a den of thieves. He drove them out of the temple so God's house could be kept sacred.

Jesus continued teaching daily in the temple and His critics including the chief priests, scribes, and leaders of the people started planning on how they could kill Him. Jesus had the support of the crowd so the leaders could not do anything to harm Jesus yet for fear of the people.

Chapter Sixteen
Jesus' Authority

Men and women with authority command others to follow orders. A president, general, ship's captain, judge, and CEO are all people of authority. They give direction to the desired destination or goal. The global economic system would quickly fail without authoritative leadership. Even churches must have strong leaders who can decide the proper actions for the congregation to be most effective.

God, Jesus, and the Holy Spirit are our authorities when it comes to spiritual matters. In olden days God spoke to the people through prophets, after Jesus ascended back to heaven the apostles spoke as directed, and today the Holy Spirit speaks to us as we seek God's will.

Jesus' Authority Questioned (Luke 20:1-8)

Jesus was teaching and preaching the Gospel in the temple when the chief priests, scribes, and Sanhedrin council came to question His authority. They wanted to know who had given Him the authority to preach and teach. Jesus oftentimes would answer a question by asking a question. He asked them if the baptism of John (*the Baptist*) was from heaven or of men.

The leaders decided if they said baptism was from heaven, Jesus would ask them why they did not believe Him. If they said baptism was of man, the people would stone them to death, for they were convinced John the Baptist was a prophet. They told Jesus they did not know the origin of baptism so they could save themselves. Jesus then told them He would not reveal by what authority He preached, taught, and performed miracles.

Parable of the Vinedressers (Luke 20:9-19)

Jesus painted a word picture to clarify His authority. A man planted a vineyard and leased it to others to tend. The owner went to another country for an extended stay. When it was time to harvest the grapes, the owner sent his aide to the tenants so they could give him his portion of the crop. The tenants beat the aide up and sent him home with no grapes for the owner. He then sent two more servants and they were abused and sent away empty-handed.

The owner decided to send his son whom he loved and hoped they would respect. The tenants reasoned they should kill the son because he was the heir to the vineyard. If they killed the son, they thought they would automatically become the eventual owners of the vineyard. They expelled the son from the vineyard and killed him. Jesus asked what the owner would do after they killed his son. Jesus said the owner would come and deal harshly with the tenants and give the vineyard to others. Those who questioned Jesus' authority said there was no way this should happen.

Jesus then told them the meaning of the parable. God sent His Son to earth to reap a harvest of souls. Jesus' enemies killed Him as if they were expelling Him from their presence. Jesus will return someday to deal harshly with all who reject Him on earth.

He said the Stone (*Christ*) the builders rejected has become the chief Stone of the corner (*cornerstone*) as prophesied in Psalm 118:22-23. Every person who falls on that Stone will be broken in pieces; but if the Stone falls on them, they will be crushed and scattered as dust. The authorities wanted to arrest Jesus at that moment, but they feared the people; for they knew the parable was against them. Jesus had put them on the defensive.

The chief priests and scribes appointed spies to keep a close eye on Jesus so they would hopefully hear Him say something that would be incriminatory. If so, they would then have grounds for His arrest. The enemy tried to entrap Jesus by asking if it was lawful to pay taxes to Caesar. Jesus was aware of their intent to entrap, so He asked them why they tempted Him. He asked them to show Him a coin. He wanted them to tell Him whose inscription and image was on the coin. They told Him it was Caesar's. Jesus told them to pay Caesar the taxes due him, and to God the things which were God's. They were amazed at how Jesus answered but they did not arrest Him.

Resurrection Questioned (Luke 20:27-39)

The Sadducees were a group of Jews who placed great importance on the material things of this world. They denied the resurrection, and the existence of angels and spirits. Sadducees also rejected the teachings and traditions of the elders.

The Sadducees asked Jesus about Moses' writing about a man who was married, and he died before the couple had children. Their question was whether the second brother should marry his widow and have children. They further complicated the scenario by asking if the second brother also died and they had not had children, if the third brother should marry the widow. They said there were seven brothers who all married the widow, but all of them died before the woman had children. Their key question was, whose wife she would she be at the resurrection (*that they denied*).

Jesus simply told them at the resurrection there will be no marriages (Luke 20:35). Furthermore, there will be no more death (*of believers*) after the resurrection as we will be equal to the angels who never die. We are sons of the resurrection as we are sons of the God of eternity. Jesus finished His statement by saying He is not the God of the dead, but of the living, for all believers live for Him. Some of the scribes said He had spoken well, so they did not dare ask any more questions.

Jesus then asked the scribes how they could say Christ was the Son of David. He said David called

Christ Lord when he said, "The Lord said unto my LORD (God), 'Sit thou on my right hand, till I (God) make thine enemies thy footstool.'" (Psalm 110:1) He asked the scribes how He could be both Lord and a Son at the same time.

Jesus then warned the crowd to be fully aware of the scribes who devoured widow' houses, and then for a show prayed long prayers in the temple. They wore long robes, greeted people in the markets, sat in the choice seats in the synagogues, and ate in the chief rooms at the feasts. Jesus said they would receive the greater damnation.

Chapter Seventeen
The Signs of the Times

Luke 21 opens with the account of the wealthy and a very poor widow in the temple. Jesus witnessed some of the wealthy giving out of pride to the temple treasury because they could give so much. Jesus saw the poor widow give a gift of only two mites to God. There were thirteen offering receptacles in the shape of a trumpet located throughout the temple where worshipers could give their tithes and offerings to God. The widow's two mites were most likely two copper coins with very little value, but it was all she had. The poor widow had given more than all the wealthy because she gave all.

The Signs of the Times (Luke 21:7-19)

Jesus spoke often of the End of the Age when God's judgment will be rendered to every person. The people asked Jesus when the End of Time would be and what forewarning signs there will be. They probably thought the same way people think about the end time today. If they got a sign or a warning before the end, they could make things right with God at the last moment; but this is not God's plan.

Jesus told the people to be on guard that they not be deceived by people who would come in His name claiming to be Christ (*anti-Christ*). He warned them to not follow after these false teachers who would lie and mislead them. He said we will hear of wars and rumors of wars, but we are not to let this distract us from God, as wars must occur before He returns to claim His church. Jesus warned we will see wars between nations, earthquakes in many countries, famines, pestilences (*plagues*), fearful sights, and great signs from heaven before the end of time.

Jesus also said believers will be arrested, persecuted, and tried before the authorities for His name's sake. Many believers will face prison time because they refuse to denounce Christ. Paul demonstrated that prison time is also a time to witness for Christ to unbelievers. He told the believers to not pre-plan what they would say when arrested because He would provide the proper words to say at the moment. The authorities would not be able to refute the words Jesus gave as a defense of the believer's faith.

He went on to say family members will testify against their loved ones who are believers. Some of the believers will be put to death because of their faith. Others will be hated because we claim Christ as our Savior. He tells us to patiently endure persecution should we have to face it. It is clear that world conditions will not improve before Jesus comes back to make all things new.

<u>Destruction Forecast</u> (Luke 21:5-6 and 21:20-24)

Jesus spoke of the beautiful and precious stones and expensive donated items used to decorate the temple interior in Jerusalem. (Luke 21:5-6) Then He warned again of the day when destruction would befall Jerusalem and one stone would not be left on top of another. The temple and the city would be utterly destroyed by their enemies.

The armies would surround Jerusalem and the citizens would know desolation and destruction was near. Jesus told them they needed to flee for safety to the mountains. Those living in the country should not come to Jerusalem lest they be stranded or killed during the siege and destruction. Christ said this must occur so the Old Testament prophecies could be fulfilled. He was especially concerned about mothers-to-be and those with new born babies that were still breast-feeding. The enemy's wrath and destruction would be very difficult if not impossible for these young women. Some would be killed while others would be taken captive to enemy countries. Jerusalem would be trampled and completely overrun by their Gentile enemies.

War always has devastating consequences. Families are torn apart and they will never be the same without their missing or dead loved ones who gave their all. We will continue to have wars until Jesus comes back to earth as our Prince of Peace.

Jesus' Return (Luke 21:25-28)

In John 14:1-3, Jesus said, "Let not your heart be troubled: ye believe in God, believe also in Me. In My Father's house are many mansions: if it were not so, I would have told you. I go to prepare a place for you. And if I go and prepare a place for you, I will come again, and receive you unto Myself, that where I am, there ye may be also." Jesus spoke to troubled people who had concerns about their future destiny after this life on earth. He calls on us to believe fully in God and Him as their promises are sure and certain. Jesus had to die so He could be resurrected with a new glorified body that ascended back to God in heaven. We will receive our new glorified body just like His on resurrection day when He comes again. Then all God's children can dwell in a perfect place of peace, happiness, and joy forever and ever; for there will be no more pain or death.

Jesus said there will be signs in the sun, moon, the stars, and on earth. Acts 2:20-21 says, "The sun shall be turned into darkness, and the moon into blood, before that great and notable day of the Lord come: and it shall come to pass, that whosoever shall call on the name of the Lord shall be saved." This reminds us of what happened on the day Jesus was crucified. Luke 22:44-45 tells us darkness was over the earth for three daylight hours. The sun was darkened and the veil of the temple was torn in two.

Joel 2:1-2 prophesied about the coming day of the Lord (*crucifixion*) that he said was at hand. It would be a day of darkness and gloom, a day of thick clouds and darkness during the morning hours. There would never be another day like this.

Luke 21:26 says men's hearts will be failing them from fear and the expectation of future coming events on earth. About twenty percent of all deaths in the USA are from heart disease. One person dies every thirty-four seconds from heart disease according to the Center for Disease Control (*CDC*). Not all heart attacks can be attributed to stress, but we know stress takes its toll on our overall health, including the heart.

One day, Jesus will step out of the clouds in grandeur and great glory as we witness His power over death and eternity. He will come in magnificence and majesty as He comes to rapture His church. We will hear the trumpet blast and a great voice from heaven and look up to see Jesus coming with all the saints and hosts of angels in the clouds. Our Redeemer will come to take us home to be with Him for eternity.

Jesus warns us in Luke 21:34-37 to be alert and watch for His soon return. He will come unexpectedly like a thief who gives no forewarning. We must not let our lives be so busy that we fail to remember His promise that He is coming back at any moment. Jesus said His coming will be like a snare or trap on the entire earth. There will be no escape from the judgment to come. Jesus instructs us to watch and pray always so we will be found faithful and worthy when He comes. We must be ready at all times to stand before Jesus on that day.

Jesus told the parable of the fig tree in Luke 21:29-33. He said when we see buds on the trees we know summer is approaching. Likewise, when we see Bible prophecies about the end time being fulfilled, we know the kingdom of God is near. He closes with the assurance that heaven and earth will melt with intense heat and pass away, but His Word will endure forever.

Chapter Eighteen
Betrayal and Denial

Jesus knew His time on earth was now very short. The scribes, Pharisees, and the majority of the Sanhedrin Council opposed His message and miracles openly. The Jews could not accept the fact that God sent Jesus from heaven to earth as His only divine Son; nor could they duplicate His miracles. Jealousy and fear ruled the opposer's hearts, and they felt Jesus' death on the cross was their only way to solve the problem He had created in the religious world. Many Jews turned from Judaism to Christianity during Christ's ministry and this added to the religious leader's concerns. They must kill Him sooner rather than later to stop this nonsense.

The Evil Plan (Luke 22:1-6)

It was time for the annual Passover Feast to be held in Jerusalem. This was a high holy day for Jews, and it still is. The feast called Seder was celebrated to remember God's deliverance of their forefathers from four hundred years of slavery in Egypt and the death angel passing over their ancestor's homes. Pharaoh refused to listen to Moses who delivered God's message to let His people go. God finally sent the plague of death to every Egyptian household that took the life of each family's first born. The death angel passed over the Israelite's homes because they had applied the blood of a lamb on the door posts and lentils.

The chief priests and scribes feared the people who believed in Jesus' teachings, but they still plotted to kill Him. Satan knew which of Jesus' twelve disciples was the weakest, so he entered Judas Iscariot, the treasurer for the disciples. Judas discussed with Jesus' enemies how he could betray Him. They gladly gave Judas a monetary bribe to carry out his cowardly act against Christ. Judas' greed for money took control of his thought process. He forfeited his love for Christ for a few coins. Judas started coming up with a plan to betray Him.

The Passover Meal (Luke 22:7-13)

The Passover Meal is very important to most Jews. It is estimated that about seventy percent of all Jews still celebrate Passover today. The meal consists of seven main dishes:

- Karpas– vegetables dipped in salt water to symbolize the Jew's sweat and tears while in slavery
- Zeroah– roasted lamb to remember the blood of the lamb their forefathers applied to their door posts and lentils so the death angel would pass over
- Beitza– a hard-boiled egg to represent mourning and a new birth
- Matzo balls stuffed with fresh herbs– represents the unleavened bread eaten during Passover, slavery, redemption, and faith in God
- Maror and Hazeret– bitter herbs and vegetables to represent bitter slavery and ultimate freedom
- Haroset– a mixture of apples, nuts, and grape juice to recall the mixture used to make Pharaoh's bricks, but also sweet release and redemption.

Passover was a time to celebrate deliverance by God from slavery, freedom, faith in God, prayer, new life, and service to God.

It was now time for Jesus to eat His final Passover meal with His twelve disciples. The Passover lamb must be slain and roasted and the other menu ingredients purchased. Jesus sent Peter and John to find a location and prepare the Passover so they could eat together. He told them to go into the city and they would see a man carrying a pitcher of water. Jesus told them to follow the man into his house and tell him Jesus wanted to use his guest room so He they could eat the Passover meal. Jesus told them the man would show them a large, furnished upper room, and to get the meal ready. It is amazing how Jesus knows every detail we need to meet His standards and obey His commands.

The Lord's Supper (Luke 22:14-23)

This Passover Meal would be different from the others the disciples had shared with Jesus previously. The apostles met with Jesus in the upper room where He told them He had been looking forward to this special meal before going to the cross. He said He would not have another Passover with them until it is fulfilled in God's kingdom. Jesus would offer Himself at the cross as our atoning sacrifice and as our unblemished Lamb. All believers will receive the full benefits and blessings of His sacrifice when He returns to earth with all the saints who have died in the Lord.

Jesus then instituted what we refer to as the Lord's Supper. He took the cup of grape juice and blessed it, and He said, "Take this, and divide it among yourselves: for I say unto you, I will not drink of the fruit of the vine until the kingdom of God shall come." This must have been a bittersweet time for Jesus, as He knew the cross would be His destiny the next day.

He took the unleavened bread and gave thanks. He said, "This is my body which is given for you: this do in remembrance of me." He said the cup is the New Testament in His blood, which would be shed for each of them. Jesus wanted His disciples to share in His death, but also remember His final redemptive work. Jesus gives us a new covenant when He takes away our sins, to remember them no more. His blood was shed for every believer who will accept His forgiveness as our Lord.

Jesus said in 1 Corinthians 11:26, "For as often as ye eat this bread, and drink this cup, ye do show the Lord's death till he comes." When we partake of the Lord's Supper, it is a time for self-examination. (1 Corinthians 11:28) We ask God to mend any brokenness in our spiritual lives so we can enjoy a close communion with Him. We need to remember His sacrifice and victory over death often.

Then Jesus announced that His betrayer was at the table with Him. Jesus said, "Woe unto that man by whom He is betrayed." Judas would pay a heavy price for betraying His Lord. The disciples began asking who it was that would betray Him.

Selfish Argument (Luke 22:24-30)

The disciples chose a very bad time to have a silly argument. They had just celebrated their final Passover meal with Jesus and partook of the first Lord's Supper. This shows how Satan can create confusion at the most inappropriate time. They argued who would be the greatest disciple in their group. Some of the disciples wanted to be supreme over the others. This was a teaching opportunity for Jesus. He told them the Gentiles liked to rule over others, but not so among them. Jesus told them that if they wanted to be superior, to humble themselves like the youngest disciple. Jesus was facing death on the cross while they wanted a promotion. He was getting ready to show how humble He was by going to the cross. Jesus came to humbly serve all mankind by paying our debt of sin through His brutal death.

The disciples would start sharing in God's kingdom as soon as Jesus was resurrected and ascended back to God in heaven. He told them they will sit at His table to eat and drink in His kingdom. The apostles will sit on thrones to judge the twelve tribes of Israel.

Denial (Luke 22:31-34)

Jesus knew He would be betrayed by Judas, for this fulfilled Old Testament prophecy. Sometimes God's foreordained plan includes pain, suffering, and even death. Jesus was facing a very excruciating execution on the cross the next day. He had a special message for Peter that night. He told Peter Satan would sift him like wheat, but Jesus prayed for Peter that his faith would not fail. Jesus knew Peter would fall away from Him that night through his denial of knowing Him. He told Peter when he returned to the other disciples to strengthen them. Peter told Jesus he would go with Him to prison and death. Jesus told Peter he would deny knowing Him three times before the rooster crowed in the morning.

In Luke 22:54-62, we are told about Peter's denial of knowing Christ. Jesus was betrayed by Judas Iscariot and arrested by the soldiers. (Luke 22:47-53) They brought Jesus to the high priest's house as Peter followed in the darkness at a distance. Some of the witnesses gathered in a courtyard nearby and built a fire to keep warm. As Peter sat among the people, a servant girl looked at Peter and told him he was with Jesus. Peter denied knowing Christ as he frankly told the girl he did not know Christ (*first denial*).

Someone else saw Peter a little later that night and said Peter was one of them (*Jesus' disciples*). Peter told the man emphatically he was not one of the disciples (*second denial*). About an hour later, another man said Peter was one of the disciples as he was from Galilee. Peter told the man he didn't know what he was saying (*third denial*). While Peter was still speaking, a rooster crowed just as Jesus predicted. Jesus was nearby and heard Peter's denial. Jesus looked intently at Peter and he then remembered what Jesus had predicted. He went out and wept bitterly for letting his Lord down.

Jesus reminded His disciples they had gone out purely on faith during His three-year ministry.

They didn't take any personal clothing or items they would need daily, they didn't take money or sandals, and yet their daily needs were met. Jesus then predicted His upcoming suffering and said He was numbered among the transgressors like a criminal. (Isaiah 53:12) His earthly ministry was quickly drawing to a close as tomorrow would be His fateful day on Calvary.

<u>Jesus' Agonizing Prayer</u> (Luke 22:39-46)

Jesus often went to the Mount of Olives to be alone with God and pray. His ministry was very taxing and He needed to stay in close touch with God who supplied strength and power. His disciples followed Him to the private place of prayer that night. Three of His disciples went a little further with Jesus where He told them to stay there while He went into the garden to pray. He told His disciples to also pray that they would not enter into temptation.

Jesus knelt and prayed that God would remove the cup of suffering (*death on the cross*) if that was God's will. Jesus knew the suffering and pain when someone was crucified, so it is natural that He wanted to avoid the cross if that was God's will. Jesus finally surrendered His will to God and asked that God's will be done. He prayed earnestly and His sweat became as great drops of blood that fell to the ground. Jesus finally came back to His three disciples and found them sleeping. He told them to get up and pray so they would not be tempted.

Jesus must have felt a sense of relief when He surrendered His will to God. He knew what lay ahead was going to be very painful, but He had an overriding desire to do what the Father wanted. God's foreordained plan was for Jesus to shed His blood to pay our sin debt. Jesus already knew He would come forth in victory over death on the third day after He was crucified.

<u>Betrayal and Arrest</u> (Luke 22:47-53)

As Jesus talked with His three disciples, Judas and the soldiers came to Jesus with torches, clubs, and swords in the darkness of night. Judas kissed Jesus, and He asked Judas if he was betraying Him with a kiss. The disciples wanted to draw their swords to defend Jesus. Peter cut off the right ear of one of the high priest's servants. Jesus performed His final earthly miracle by healing the man's ear. Jesus then asked the soldiers if they came with swords and clubs to arrest Him like a robber. They had not arrested Jesus previously when He taught in the temple, but He knew the hour had now come. The betrayal and arrest were a part of God's plan for Jesus to be arrested and taken to the authorities.

<u>Interrogations and Abuse</u> (Luke 22:63-71)

The soldiers were in control. They treated Him with contempt, ridiculed, and beat (*flogged*) Him while He was tied to a whipping post. Jesus' punishment was just beginning as it would get much worse throughout the night. They placed a blindfold on Him and then asked Him who struck Him. The soldiers insulted Him with slandering and evil words throughout the night.

The next morning, Jesus was brought to the Sanhedrin council, elders, chief priests, and scribes. They commanded Jesus to say He was the Messiah if that was the case. Jesus answered them that if He told them, they would not believe. Jesus told them if He questioned them, they would not answer either. Jesus then said from this time on, He would be seated at the right hand of God as prophesied in Psalm 110:1. The rulers then asked Him if He was the Son of God, and He answered, "It is just as you say. I AM." The rulers felt they had all the evidence they needed to proceed toward crucifixion.

Chapter Nineteen
The Cross and Final Victory

The entire audience who heard the conclusion by the rulers delivered Jesus to Pontius Pilate, the Roman governor. The religious leaders did not want to pass sentence so they passed the responsibility to the Roman government for sentencing. The rulers told Pilate Jesus had been misleading, corrupting, and turning their nation away. They lied and claimed He discouraged the people to not pay taxes to Caesar, making this an offense against the Roman government. They told Pilate Jesus claimed to be Christ the Messiah, an Anointed One, and a King.

Pilate asked Jesus if He was the King of the Jews, and Jesus answered, "It is just as you say." Pilate told the rulers he found no fault or crime in Jesus. The rulers insisted that Jesus stirred up and excited the people with His teachings throughout all Judea, from Galilee to Jerusalem. Pilate asked Jesus if He was from Galilee and Jesus said He was.

Pilate knew that Herod, whose jurisdiction included Galilee, was in Jerusalem. Pilate did not find grounds to pass sentence on Jesus, so he decided to pass Jesus off to Herod for a decision. Herod had more authority so he should be the one to make a final decision on Jesus' fate.

Herod was excited to meet Jesus since he had heard of all the miracles He had performed during His ministry. He had wanted to see Jesus for quite some time, and now at last he could meet Him in person. Herod was hoping to see some striking evidence or spectacular performance done by Jesus in his presence. Herod asked Jesus many questions, but Jesus did not respond. (Isaiah 53:7) The rulers stood by as they continued to accuse Jesus of wrongdoing. Herod and his soldiers mistreated Jesus with contempt and ridicule. They put a purple robe on Jesus like He was an earthly king. Herod then sent Jesus back to Pilate without passing sentence.

Pilate called together the chief priests, the rulers, and the people. He told them again he found no crime or guilt in Jesus based on their accusations. He found no reason to sentence Jesus to death based on their false charges. Pilate reminded the people that Herod found no reason to put Jesus to death. Jesus had done nothing to deserve death. Pilate said he would punish Jesus, teach Him a lesson, and then release Him.

By law and custom, it was necessary for Pilate to release one prisoner at the Passover Feast, so he wanted to release Jesus. The people shouted that Pilate should release Barabbas who was imprisoned for rioting and murder. They shouted against Jesus, "Crucify Him, crucify Him." Pilate insisted for the third time he found no fault in Jesus because He had done no wrong. He insisted again that he would teach Jesus a lesson through punishment and release Him. The angry crowd insisted and demanded Jesus should be crucified. Pilate gave into the people's demands and sentenced Jesus to die on the cross. He released a murderer from prison so the innocent Lamb of God could die on the cross.

The soldiers led Jesus away carrying the crossbeam for his cross. The vertical pole for the crossbeam was already at the crucifixion site on Calvary's hill. Jesus had been flogged with a whip at the whipping post and abused, so He did not have the physical strength to bear such a heavy load. Simon of Cyrene was visiting Jerusalem, so the soldiers told him to carry Jesus' cross to Calvary. A large crowd followed Jesus through the narrow streets to His crucifixion site outside Jerusalem.

Several women were in the crowd and they wept loudly because of Jesus' abuse and death sentence. Jesus turned and told the women to not weep for Him, but weep for themselves and their children. He said the day would come when barren women would be blessed by not having children when Jerusalem would fall to the enemy. The people would cry out for the mountains to fall on them when destruction came to the city.

God's chosen people in Jerusalem would suffer much because of their rejection of Jesus and His salvation. When Jesus was with them, the time was right to find salvation, but many refused.

Two criminals were led with Jesus to be crucified. A criminal was on each side of Jesus' cross. The place was called Golgotha in Aramaic because the hill resembled a skull. In Latin the crucifixion hill was called Calvary (*a skull*). The Romans commonly used this location for crucifixion of criminals outside the city walls. When they hung Jesus on the cross, He prayed, "Father, forgive them, for they know not what they do." Jesus prayed for forgiveness of those who mistreated Him the most.

The people stood watching this awful sight. The rulers mocked Jesus and sneered as they said, "He saved others; let Him save Himself if He is the Christ, the chosen of God." Their mockery made light of His divinity. The soldiers cast lots and gambled for Jesus' garments while He suffered and died. The soldiers also mocked Jesus by offering Him sour wine vinegar. The soldiers challenged Jesus to save Himself if He was the King of the Jews. A sign was prepared for Jesus' cross. It was written in Greek, Latin, and Hebrew, and it said, "THIS IS THE KING OF THE JEWS." They attached the sign on the cross. They went out of their way to mock Jesus' claim that He was the Messiah, the Son of God.

One of the criminals also mocked Jesus by saying, "If you are the Christ, save yourself and us." The other criminal told the one who mocked and asked, "Do you not even fear God, seeing you are under the same condemnation? And we indeed justly, for we receive the due reward of our deeds; but this Man has done nothing wrong." Then he asked Jesus to remember him when He came into His kingdom. Jesus tenderly told the criminal, "Assuredly, I say to you, today you will be with Me in Paradise." Christ had a forgiving spirit for sinners until His final breath.

Darkness fell on all the earth from noon until three in the afternoon. The sun darkened and the veil at the Holy of Holies in the temple was torn in two. Jesus finally cried out loudly, "It is finished. Father, into Your hands I commit My spirit," and He died. God's plan for Jesus to shed His blood for all sinners was now finished.

The Gentile centurion, commander of a squadron of soldiers at the cross, said, "Indeed, without question, this was a righteous Man." The entire crowd who had been watching this spectacle beat their breasts and went home. The women who followed Jesus from Galilee stood at a distance as they watched and mourned with broken hearts.

Burial (Luke 23:50-56)

Joseph of Arimathea was a member of the Sanhedrin council. He had disagreed with Jesus' crucifixion as he was a good and just man since he was in right standing with God and man. Joseph was expecting and waiting for the kingdom of God to come. He went to Pilate and asked for the body of Jesus so He could have a proper burial. He removed Jesus' body from the cross, wrapped Him in burial linen cloth, and laid His body in his new and unused tomb. It was Friday, the day of preparation for the Sabbath that would commence at sundown. The women who followed Jesus now followed Joseph to the tomb so they would know where Jesus' body was entombed. They prepared burial spices, ointments, and perfumes that day. When the Sabbath began, they rested according to the Law given to Moses.

Victory (Luke 24:1-12)
During His ministry, Jesus had told His disciples repeatedly that He would die but come forth from death on the third day after He died. They had difficulty understanding what Jesus said.

The soldiers crucified Jesus on Friday. The Sabbath ended at sundown Saturday, and it is now early morning of the third day on Sunday. The women who followed and adored Jesus arrived at the tomb early that morning to anoint Jesus' body with the spices, ointments, and perfumes they prepared on Friday afternoon. When they arrived at the tomb, the heavy stone to the doorway was rolled back. They entered the tomb, but Jesus' body wasn't there. They were puzzled on where someone had taken His body.

Two men in dazzling robes suddenly stood beside the women in the tomb. The women were afraid and looked to the ground. The men asked the women why they looked for the living among the dead. The angels said, "He is not here, but is risen!" They reminded the women what Jesus had said while He was still in Galilee. He had told them, "The Son of Man must be delivered into the hands of sinful men, and be crucified, and the third day rise again." The women now remembered what He had said.

The women went and told about their experience at the tomb to the eleven disciples and others. The group of women included Mary Magdalene, Joanna, the mother of Jesus and James, and other women. The disciples could not believe what the women told them about the message from the angelic men. What they said made no sense in spite of what Jesus had said earlier in Galilee.

Peter ran to the tomb, stooped down, and looked inside. He saw the linen cloths alone by themselves. He left the tomb wondering and marveling at what had occurred.

The Emmaus Road (Luke 24:13-27)

Two of Jesus' disciples left their hiding place in Jerusalem and headed to a small village called Emmaus, about seven miles from the city. They were discussing the crucifixion and the rumor of Jesus' resurrection as they walked. Jesus suddenly appeared with them, but they did not know Him. Jesus had received His new glorified body when He was resurrected. Jesus asked them what they were discussing before He arrived. They seemed so sad. Cleopas asked Jesus if he was visiting Jerusalem, and if He did not know what had happened recently in the city. Jesus asked them, "What things?" They told Him how the rulers had crucified Jesus three days ago even though He was from God. They told Jesus about the angels and the women who reported Jesus is risen. They told Him how Peter ran to the tomb, but Jesus was not there.

Jesus told the two disciples in Luke 24:25-26, "O fools, and slow of heart to believe all that the prophets have spoken: ought not Christ to have suffered these things, and to enter into His glory?" Jesus reminded them of all the prophecies from Moses and all the prophets, concerning Him. The men still did not realize they were talking with Jesus.

As they neared Emmaus, Jesus told them He was going on further. The two disciples urged Jesus to stay with them because nightfall was coming. Jesus went inside with them. The three men reclined at a dining table where Jesus took a loaf of bread, praised God, gave thanks, and blessed it. He broke the bread and gave it to them. Their eyes were instantly opened and they recognized Jesus. He then vanished from their presence.

The two disciples returned to Jerusalem to meet the other disciples and let them know about their encounter with their risen Lord. They said the Lord is risen and He appeared to Simon Peter. They told the details of Jesus suddenly appearing with them while they walked toward Emmaus and how He broke bread with them to reveal who He was. Suddenly Jesus appeared with ten of His disciples (*Thomas was not there*) and told them, "Peace be unto you." The disciples were afraid and thought a spirit had appeared in their midst. Jesus asked them why they were troubled and had doubts and questions.

He showed them the nail scars in His hands and feet to prove He was their risen Lord. He told them to touch Him so they would know He was not just a spirit. They were filled with joy and elation knowing He arose from the dead just as He promised. Jesus asked them if they had anything to eat, and they gave Him a piece of broiled fish that He ate.

Jesus turned their attention back to the Scriptures so their minds would be open to a thorough understanding of God's plan. He referred to the references and prophecies about Him in the Old Testament including the Law, the Prophets, and the Psalms. He reminded them of the Scriptures that said the Messiah should suffer and arise from the dead on the third day.

He came, died, and arose from the dead so the message of repentance of sin and forgiveness could be preached in His name to all nations beginning in Jerusalem.

Jesus then told the disciples He would send them forth shortly into the world (*as apostles and missionaries*), but they were to remain in Jerusalem until they received power from the Holy Spirit to teach, preach, baptize, and heal.

Jesus took them out toward Bethany, lifted up His hands, and invoked a blessing on them. Jesus then left His disciples as He ascended into heaven where He sits today at the Father's right hand making intercession for us. The disciples joyfully went back to Jerusalem as they worshiped Christ and exalted God in the temple.

This book concludes with the key verse in Luke 1:4:

> "That you mightest know the certainty of those things, wherein thou hast been instructed."

We accept the writings of Luke with assurance and confidence that what he wrote was divinely inspired for our edification and learning.

Closing Thoughts

God told Adam he could eat from all the fruit trees in the Garden of Eden, but to not eat of the fruit from the one tree in the center of the garden. God told Adam and Eve if they ate the forbidden fruit they would die. They disobeyed God and listened to Satan's lie. Because of their disobedience, we all now face an earthly death sentence.

God sent His only Son Jesus from heaven to earth to reconcile man back to God. He was crucified, raised from the dead, and given a new glorified body that will never suffer or die. He ascended back to God in heaven, and now we await His return to rapture His church. We will receive a new glorified body just like His on resurrection day.

All sin, sorrows, and death will be no more. There will be no more pain or tears when we go to our eternal home. All sinful things and Satan will be banished from God's presence, and we will live forever in peace, joy, happiness, elation, and praise to God.

About the Author

Don was born at home in Tazewell County, Virginia. His dad was a coal miner and his mother worked hard to raise five children. Our parents had a strong work ethic matched by a tenacious faith in God. Even though resources were limited, our family was rich in love for the Lord and each other.

Don went to business school after graduating from high school. He worked his way through a maze of different jobs from entry level to management. His jobs ranged from administrative positions to vice president of a furniture manufacturer. Then he went into field sales calling on the military and universities. He was blessed as many doors closed, but just as many better ones were opened by the Lord.

Don has always been blessed to be fully involved in the Lord's work. For many years, he worked in the areas of music, administration, and teaching the Bible. In October 2014, his elders asked him to become the minister of his church and he still holds this position.

His family has gone through several deaths just as others have experienced, but God continues to bless. We have the blessed hope of Jesus' return to earth when families will be re-united and we will forever be with the Lord. We eagerly await His return when all things will be made new.